WORLD BANK STUDY

The Education System in the Russian Federation

Education Brief 2012

Denis Nikolaev
Dmitry Chugunov

THE WORLD BANK
Washington, D.C.

© 2012 International Bank for Reconstruction and Development / International Development Association or
The World Bank
1818 H Street NW
Washington DC 20433
Telephone: 202-473-1000
Internet: www.worldbank.org

1 2 3 4   15 14 13 12

World Bank Studies are published to communicate the results of the Bank's work to the development community with the least possible delay. The manuscript of this paper therefore has not been prepared in accordance with the procedures appropriate to formally-edited texts.

This volume is a product of the staff of The World Bank with external contributions. The findings, interpretations, and conclusions expressed in this volume do not necessarily reflect the views of The World Bank, its Board of Executive Directors, or the governments they represent.

The World Bank does not guarantee the accuracy of the data included in this work. The boundaries, colors, denominations, and other information shown on any map in this work do not imply any judgment on the part of The World Bank concerning the legal status of any territory or the endorsement or acceptance of such boundaries.

Rights and Permissions

The material in this work is subject to copyright. Because The World Bank encourages dissemination of its knowledge, this work may be reproduced, in whole or in part, for noncommercial purposes as long as full attribution to the work is given.

For permission to reproduce any part of this work for commercial purposes, please send a request with complete information to the Copyright Clearance Center Inc., 222 Rosewood Drive, Danvers, MA 01923, USA; telephone: 978-750-8400; fax: 978-750-4470; Internet: www.copyright.com.

All other queries on rights and licenses, including subsidiary rights, should be addressed to the Office of the Publisher, The World Bank, 1818 H Street NW, Washington, DC 20433, USA; fax: 202-522-2422; e-mail: pubrights@worldbank.org.

ISBN (paper): 978-0-8213-9514-1
ISBN (electronic): 978-0-8213-9515-8
DOI: 10.1596/978-0-8213-9514-1

Library of Congress Cataloging-in-Publication Data has been requested.

Contents

Acknowledgments ix
Introduction xi

1. **Country Context** 1
   Organization of the Education System 1
   Public Spending on Education 1

2. **Preschool Education and Early Childhood Development** 6
   Current Situation and Trends 6
   Recent and Ongoing Reforms 12
   Key Problems and Challenges 15
   Policy Options 16

3. **Primary and Secondary Education** 19
   Current Situation and Trends 19
   Recent and Ongoing Reforms 29
   Key Problems and Challenges 33
   Policy Options 36

4. **Vocational Education and Training** 39
   Current Situation and Trends 39
   Recent and Ongoing Reforms 44
   Key Problems and Challenges 45
   Policy Options 46

5. **Higher Education** 48
   Current Situation and Trends 48
   Recent and Ongoing Reforms 56
   Key Problems and Challenges 57
   Policy Options 59

6. **Lifelong Learning** 61
   Condition and Development Trends 61
   State Policy 63
   Staff Training (Financing and Coverage) 64
   Socially Deprived Groups of People 67
   Policy Options 68

7. **Appendixes** 73
   Appendix A. Reference Statistics—Nonfinance 75
   Appendix B. Reference Statistics—Finance 81

Figures

Figure 1.1. Structure of the education system in the Russian Federation..........................2
Figure 1.2. Structure of education financing in the Russian Federation 3
Figure 1.3. Public spending on education in the Russian Federation as a share of GDP, by level of education (percent) 3
Figure 1.4. Total public spending on education as a share of GDP and total public expenditures in the Russian Federation (percent) (2003–10) 4
Figure 1.5. Distribution of OECD and partner countries by GDP per capita and share of expenditures allocated to education in terms of GDP (including private investments in education) (2006) 4
Figure 2.1. Birth rate projections in the Russian Federation (per 1,000 inhabitants) 6
Figure 2.2. Gross enrollment to preschool educational institutions in the Russian Federation by type of settlement (adjusted for 5-to-6-year-olds studying in primary school) (2000–10, percent) 7
Figure 2.3. Number of children in preschool educational institutions and number of 1-to-6-year-olds in the Russian Federation (2000–10, thousand persons) 7
Figure 2.4. Distribution of preschool educational institutions in the Russian Federation by type of settlement (thousand units, 2000–09) 8
Figure 2.5. Distribution of staff in preschool educational institutions in the Russian Federation by position (percent) 9
Figure 2.6. Dynamics of student-teacher ratio in the Russian Federation in preschool education (persons, 1992–2010) 9
Figure 2.7. Total public expenditure in the Russian Federation on education as percent of GDP, at pre-primary level of education (ISCED 0) (2008) 10
Figure 2.8. Total public spending (top chart) and per student expenditure (bottom chart) in preschool education in the Russian Federation 11
Figure 2.9. Public expenditure on preschool education in the Russian Federation (real spending from consolidated budget, percent) (2003–10) 12
Figure 2.10. Distribution of regions in the Russian Federation by GRP per capita and enrollment to preschool education (2009) 13
Figure 2.11. Distribution of autonomous institutions in the Russian Federation by sphere (top chart) and distribution of autonomous institutions in education sphere (bottom chart) (2010) 14
Figure 2.12. Number of births in the Russian Federation (million newborns) 16
Figure 3.1. Gross coverage ratio at primary and secondary education levels and overall in the Russian Federation (2000–08) 19
Figure 3.2. Distribution of students studying in primary and secondary schools (face-to-face) by type of settlement in the Russian Federation (million persons, 2000–10) 20
Figure 3.3. Distribution of primary and secondary schools in the Russian Federation by type of settlement (thousand units, 2000–10) 20
Figure 3.4. Distribution of primary and secondary schools in the Russian Federation by type of school (thousand units, 2000–08) 21
Figure 3.5. Dynamics of growth of gymnasium and lyceum network in the Russian Federation (units, 1992–2010) 21

Figure 3.6. Distribution of teachers in primary and secondary schools in the Russian Federation by type of settlement (thousand persons, 2000–10) 22

Figure 3.7. Distribution of school principals in primary and secondary schools in the Russian Federation by type of settlement (thousand persons, 2002/03–2009/10 school year) 22

Figure 3.8. Structure of teaching staff in Russian Federation public schools by professional experience (percent, 2008/09 school year) 23

Figure 3.9. Share of pension-age teachers in Russian Federation public schools, by type of settlement (percent, 2008/09 school year) 23

Figure 3.10. Dynamics of growth of gymnasium and lyceum network in the Russian Federation (units, 1992–2010) 23

Figure 3.11. Dynamics of student-teacher ratio in primary and secondary education the Russian Federation by type of settlement (persons, 2000–10) 24

Figure 3.12. Average class size in primary and lower secondary schools the Russian Federation (2009) 24

Figure 3.13. Public spending on general education from the consolidated budget of the Russian Federation (left axis) and per student expenditure on general education (right axis) (current and fixed 2003 prices) (2003–10) 25

Figure 3.14. Annual secondary education expenditure in the Russian Federation by educational institutions per student relative to GDP per capita (2007) 26

Figure 3.15. Total public spending and per student expenditure in primary and secondary education in the Russian Federation 27

Figure 3.16. Distribution of regions in the Russian Federation by GRP per capita and public spending on primary and secondary education (RUR, 2009) 27

Figure 3.17. Monthly schoolteacher remuneration in the Russian Federation in current and fixed prices (RUR, left axis) and ratio of teacher salary to average salary in the economy (right axis) (2000–10) 28

Figure 3.18. Distribution of regions in the Russian Federation by average wage in the regional systems of school education (RUR, current prices) 29

Figure 3.19. Comparison of regions in the Russian Federation by number of educational institutions transferred to autonomous status (2010) 33

Figure 3.20. PISA scores of students in the Russian Federation (2000, 2003, 2006, 2009) 34

Figure 4.1. Gross coverage of initial and secondary vocational education and training in the Russian Federation (percent, 2000–10) 39

Figure 4.2. Number of students in initial and secondary vocational educational institutions and number of people at age 15–17 and 17–19 in the Russian Federation (thousand persons, 2000–10) 40

Figure 4.3. Number of state initial and secondary vocational educational institutions in the Russian Federation (units, 2000–10) 40

Figure 4.4. Structure of staff in IVET institutions by position in the Russian Federation (percent) 41

Figure 4.5. Number of teaching staff in public SVET institutions in the Russian Federation (thousand persons, 2000–10) 41

Figure 4.6. Dynamics of student-teacher ratio (students to teaching staff) in initial and secondary vocational institutions in the Russian Federation (2000-10) 42

Figure 4.7. Total public spending (left axis) and per student expenditure (right axis) in vocational education in the Russian Federation 42

Figure 4.8. Public expenditure on vocational education per student as share of GDP per capita, share of total public expenditure on education, and share of total public expenditure in the Russian Federation (percent) (2003–10) 43

Figure 4.9. Distribution of regions in the Russian Federation by GRP per capita and public spending on VET (RUR, 2009) 44

Figure 4.10. Enrollment in state VET in 2010 by sources of financing in the Russian Federation (thousands persons) 44

Figure 5.1. Gross coverage by and enrollment in higher education in the Russian Federation (2000–10, percent) 48

Figure 5.2. Distribution of students in higher education institutions by type of ownership and form of education in the Russian Federation (thousand persons, 1990–2010) 49

Figure 5.3. Number of graduates from upper-secondary schools (state and private) and entrants to higher education institutions (state and private) in the Russian Federation (thousand persons, 1992–2010) 49

Figure 5.4. Distribution of entrants to higher education institutions in the Russian Federation by form of education (thousand persons, 2000–10) 50

Figure 5.5. Distribution of higher education institutions in the Russian Federation by form of ownership (units, 2000–10) 50

Figure 5.6. Distribution of public higher education institutions in the Russian Federation by level of subordination (2008/09, percent) 51

Figure 5.7. Distribution of public higher education institutions in the Russian Federation by type (2008/09, percent) 51

Figure 5.8. Distribution of staff in public higher education institutions in the Russian Federation by position (percent, school years 2000/01 and 2008/09) 52

Figure 5.9. Public spending on higher education institutions in the Russian Federation by type (RUR, 2006–08) 52

Figure 5.10. Total public spending (left axis) and per student expenditure (right axis) in higher education in the Russian Federation 53

Figure 5.11. Public expenditure on higher education in the Russian Federation per student as share of GDP per capita, as share of total public expenditure on education, and as share of total public expenditure (percent, 2003–10) 53

Figure 5.12. Per student expenditures on higher education in OECD and partner countries (2007, US$, PPP) 54

Figure 5.13. Distribution of regions in the Russian Federation by average wage in the regional higher education systems (RUR, 2009) 54

Figure 5.14. Distribution of regions in the Russian Federation by average wage in the regional higher education systems (RUR; 2002, 2005, 2010) 55

Figure 6.1. Participation in nonformal education and training in the Russian Federation (percent of total respondents aged 25–64, reference period 12 months, 2007) 61

Figure 6.2. Participation in informal education and training in the Russian Federation (percent of total respondents aged 25–64, reference period 12 months, 2007) 62

Figure 6.3. Motivation of adults to participate in lifelong learning in the Russian Federation 65
Figure 6.4. Sources of financing in lifelong learning in the Russian Federation 66
Figure 6.5. Average monthly costs of organizations for professional education per worker in the Russian Federation (US$) 66
Figure 6.6. Budgetary expenditure for retraining and upgrading qualifications in the Russian Federation (US$ million) 67

Tables

Table 2.1. Public expenditure on ECEC in the Russian Federation, 2003–10 11
Table 2.2. Distribution of autonomous institutions in the Russian Federation by sphere and subordination (data from July 1, 2010) 13
Table 3.1. Public spending on general education per one student in the regions of the Russian Federation (RUR, current prices) (2002–10) 28
Table A1. Number of students in educational institutions in the Russian Federation .. 75
Table A2. Number of educational institutions in the Russian Federation 77
Table A3. Gross coverage by education in the Russian Federation, percent (by level of education, calculations based on full-time equivalents) 79
Table A4. Ratio of students to teaching staff in the Russian Federation, by type of institution (by level of education, calculations based on full-time equivalents) 80
Table B1. Basic reference statistics in the Russian Federation 81
Table B2. Expenditures from consolidated budget of the Russian Federation (thousand RUR) 82
Table B3. Annual government expenditure in the Russian Federation by educational institutions relative to total public expenditure on education 83
Table B4. Annual government expenditure in the Russian Federation per student by educational institutions relative to GDP per capita 83

Acknowledgments

This report is the result of a collaborative effort of the World Bank Russian education team. The main authors of the report are Denis Nikolaev and Dmitry Chugunov, education consultants for the World Bank. Of greatest importance are the preceding reports for 2009 and 2010, prepared with the assistance of Isak Froumin (Lead Education Specialist), Kirill Vasiliev (Education Specialist), and Tigran Shmis (Education Specialist) and their helpful comments during 2012 report development. The team is indebted to Irina Reshetnikova and Julia Sazonova for team assistance. Special thanks are owed to Tobias Linden (Lead Education Specialist) and Xiaonan Cao (Knowledge and Learning Coordinator) for reviewing this report and for making suggestions for its improvement. The report was finalized under the helpful guidance of Soren Nellemann (Senior Education Specialist and Russia HD CSC). Full responsibility for errors and misinterpretations remains, however, with the authors.

Denis Nikolaev
Dmitry Chugunov

Introduction

This study is intended for non-Russian researchers wanting to get familiar with the education system of the Russian Federation and more generally for all those involved in education and education policy. It does not represent exhaustive information on the Russian education system and all problems and challenges existing there, but briefly describes its main features.

The Education System in the Russian Federation: Education Brief 2012 retains its main special feature, which is the combination of statistical data and qualitative information to describe the organization and functioning of the Russian education system.

The study provides an up-to-date array of indicators to measure the current state of education in the country. The indicators provide information on the human and financial resources invested in education, and on how education and learning subsystems operate and evolve.

The analytical parts of the report examine key problems and challenges faced by education system administrators and policy makers in the education sphere.

The report has the following structure. The opening chapter provides an overview of the education system in Russia and briefly reviews the most evident emergent trends. Chapters 2 through 5 are devoted to description of education system by level. The chapters are arranged by ascending order of educational level and each chapter presents information in a progression from the most general to the most specific. First, data on the current state of education system is provided. They characterize the human and financial resources allocated to education, describe the network of educational institutions across the country, and show regional disparities of spending on education. Next in each section key problems and challenges are examined; the focus is mainly made on access to and quality of educational services. Third, information on recent and ongoing reforms in the education sphere addresses each subsector separately and defines features typical for each of them. Fourth, there is discussion of policy options and analysis of what can be improved in the Russian education sphere.

Finally, section 6 is devoted to lifelong learning. First, the section focuses on the condition of and development trends in lifelong learning. Then it examines the state of policy, staff training including financing and coverage, and learning for socially deprived groups of people. The section concludes with policy options and possible measures for improvement.

CHAPTER 1

Country Context

Organization of the Education System

Figure 1.1 gives an overview of the education system in Russia for mainstream schooling from the pre-primary level up to higher education. The figure excludes post-graduate level education and doctoral studies.[1]

At the pre-primary level, children are admitted into the school system from the ages of 1 to 6. Compulsory education starts at the age of 6 (6 years and 6 month according to Russian legislation[2]) and generally corresponds to entry into primary school. Beginning from September 1, 2007 compulsory full-time education lasts for eleven years and continues up to the age of 17. The general education school system of Russia consists of nine years of basic general education (primary and lower secondary education) and two years of upper secondary education, which leads to the certification of complete secondary education. Basic general education is almost always provided in single-structure schools without a transition between primary and lower secondary levels, up to the age of 15. The end of basic general education coincides with the transition between lower and upper secondary education.

There are two main options in upper-secondary education:[3] the general education option, which prepares the pupils for higher education, and the vocational option, which prepares pupils both for working life and for higher education. These different options are organized into separate programs and institutions, and the students have to opt for one or the other.

In 2003 Russia signed the Bologna Declaration, which launched the process of migrating from Russian traditional tertiary education model to a modern degree structure in line with Bologna Process model. In October 2007 in Russia a law was enacted that replaced the traditional five-year model of education with a two-tiered approach: a four-year bachelor degree followed by a two-year master's degree. In 2010 the admission to the traditional five-year programs was stopped. By 2014, in Russia there should be no five-year programs students excluding just a few specializations.

Public Spending on Education

The structure of educational financing in Russia has changed during recent decade with little changes at preschool and vocational levels (1–2 percent fluctuation) and rather dramatic increase/decrease at higher/primary and secondary levels (figure 1.2).

Figure 1.1. Structure of the education system in the Russian Federation

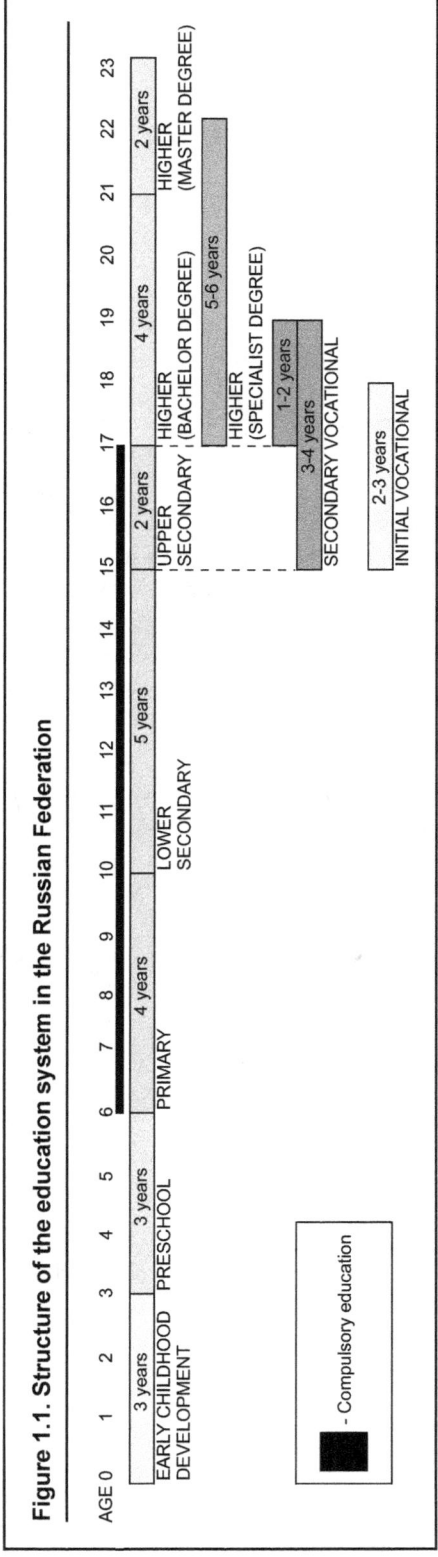

Source: Authors' estimations based on information of Ministry of Education and Science of the Russian Federation.

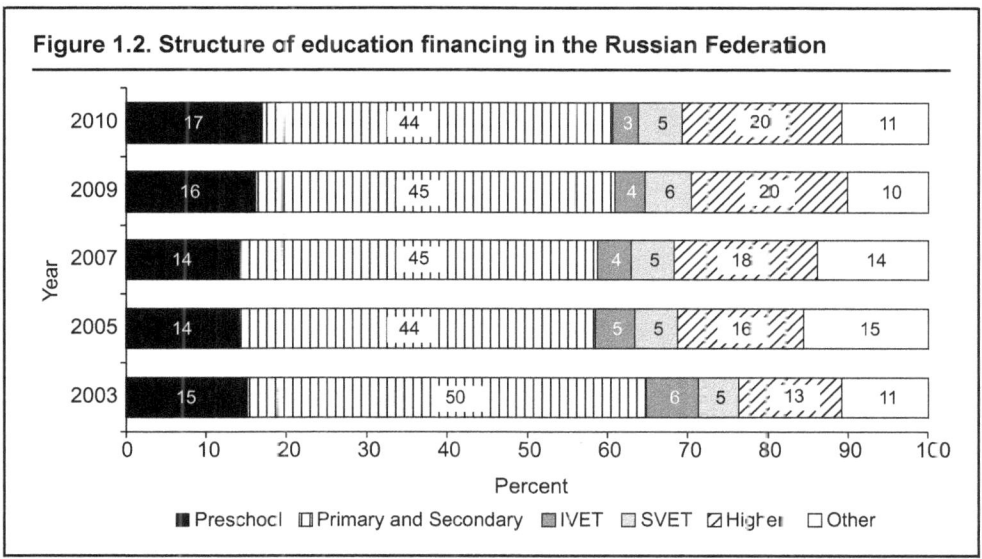

Figure 1.2. Structure of education financing in the Russian Federation

Source: Authors' calculations based on data of the Treasury of the Russian Federation.
Note: Figure shows share of expenditures in the total government spending on education, by level (2003, 2005, 2007, 2009, 2010). IVET = initial vocational education and training. SVET = secondary vocational education and training.

Public expenditure on education by educational level differs. The total public expenditure on education allocated to primary and secondary (general) education represents a greater proportion of GDP than expenditure on other educational levels but never goes above 2.0 percent (in 2009) (figure 1.3).

The share of public expenditures allocated to education sector states is approximately 11–12 percent; it reached its maximum in 2004 (12.7 percent) and then slightly dropped to 10.9 percent in 2010. But in terms of country GDP the share of public expen-

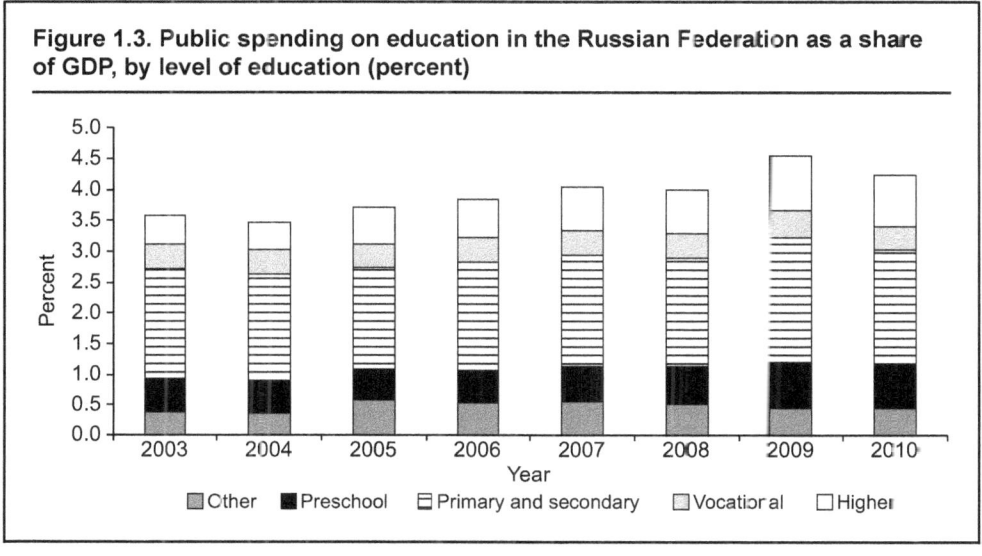

Figure 1.3. Public spending on education in the Russian Federation as a share of GDP, by level of education (percent)

Source: Authors' calculations based on the data of Treasury of the Russian Federation, and Federal Service for State Statistics of the Russian Federation.

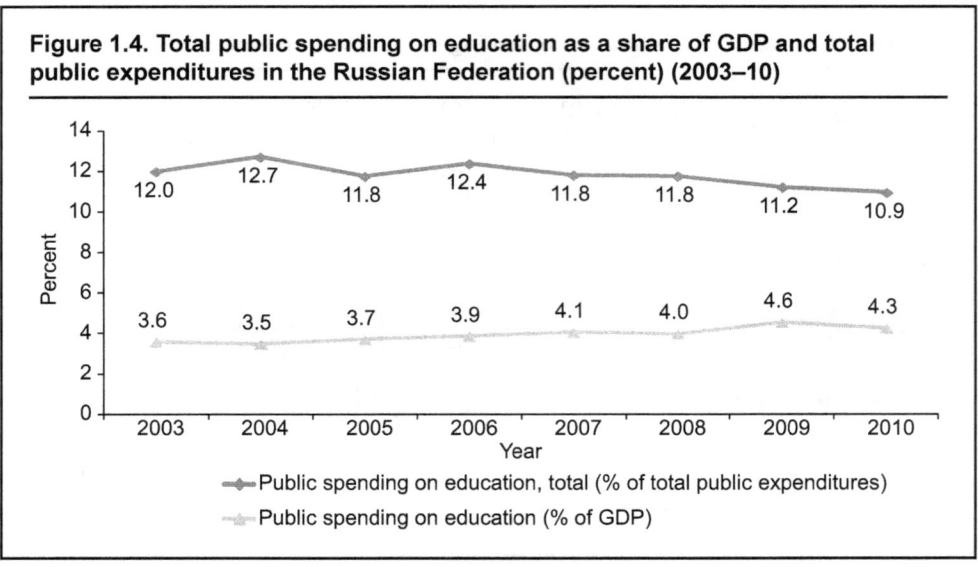

Figure 1.4. Total public spending on education as a share of GDP and total public expenditures in the Russian Federation (percent) (2003–10)

Source: Authors' calculations based on the data of Treasury of the Russian Federation, and Federal Service for State Statistics of the Russian Federation.

ditures on education is growing: it has increased from 3.6 percent in 2003 to 4.3 percent in 2010 (figure 1.4). This is a result of highly raised public expenditures within slow growth of GDP.

The ratio of education expenditures to a country's GDP defines the share of national wealth that a country spends on its education system. Russia spends on education the same part of its GDP as countries with similar economic development—5.5 percent of GDP in 2006 (expenditures include private investments in education). By international comparison that indicator varies from 3 percent in Turkey to 8 percent in Iceland (figure 1.5).

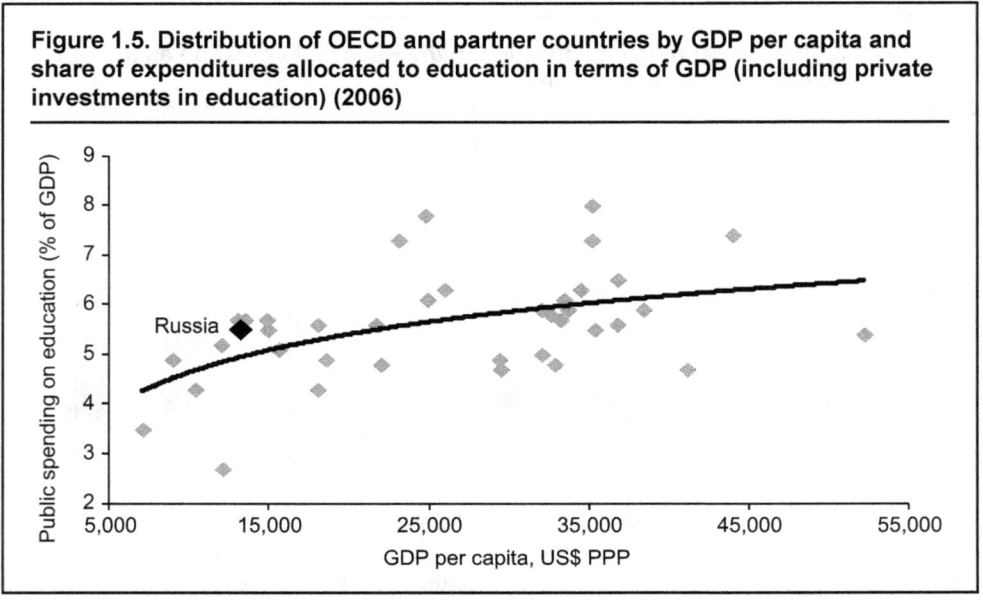

Figure 1.5. Distribution of OECD and partner countries by GDP per capita and share of expenditures allocated to education in terms of GDP (including private investments in education) (2006)

Source: Authors' calculations based on the data of Agranovich and Kovaleva, 2010.

Notes

1. According to Russian legislation post-graduate education and doctoral studies in Russia are not considered as formal stages of education, but as science activity.
2. According to Federal Law on Education.
3. In practice there are more options. For example, students after completion of upper-secondary education may go straight to the labor market.

References

Abdrahmanova, G., Gohberg, L., Zabaturina, I., Kovaleva, G., Kovaleva, N., Kuznetsova, V., Ozerova, O., Shuvalova, O. 2010. *Education in the Russian Federation: 2010.* Annual Statistical Publication. Higher School of Economics. Moscow: State University, Higher School of Economics.

Agranovich M., Kovaleva G. 2010. "Russian Education in the Context of International Indicators." Analytical report, Moscow.

Russian Federation. 1992. Federal Law of the Russian Federation from July 10, 1992 N3266-1 "On Education" (with edits from December 27, 2009).

CHAPTER 2

Preschool Education and Early Childhood Development

Current Situation and Trends

Coverage and Demography

According to data published by the Russian Federal State Statistics Service, the birth rate has grown year-on-year since 2006 by an estimated 8.3 percent, reaching currently 12.5 per 1,000 of population (see figure 2.1), and is now greater than the European Union average of 9.90 per 1,000 people (2010). The Russian Ministry of Health and Social Affairs announced that in 2010, the population of Russia had increased; at the same time the birth rate had not yet equalized with the annual death rate. The population increased due to growth of in-migration. However, fertility is increasing and mortality continues to decline in Russia. By far the largest concentration of population is in Moscow, a city of more than 10 million inhabitants.

Attendance at a preschool establishment is optional in Russia; parents are free to enroll their child if they wish. However, the state is obliged to provide parents with the services if they are requested.[1] High demand in preschool services generates inequalities in this area—coverage by preschool services varies from 9 percent to 86 percent among Russian regions. Average coverage of preschool educational institutions of children at the age of 1–7 in Russia was 52 percent in 2000. The situation has insignificantly improved in recent years: in 2010 59.4 percent of preschool age children were covered by services in preschool educational institutions.

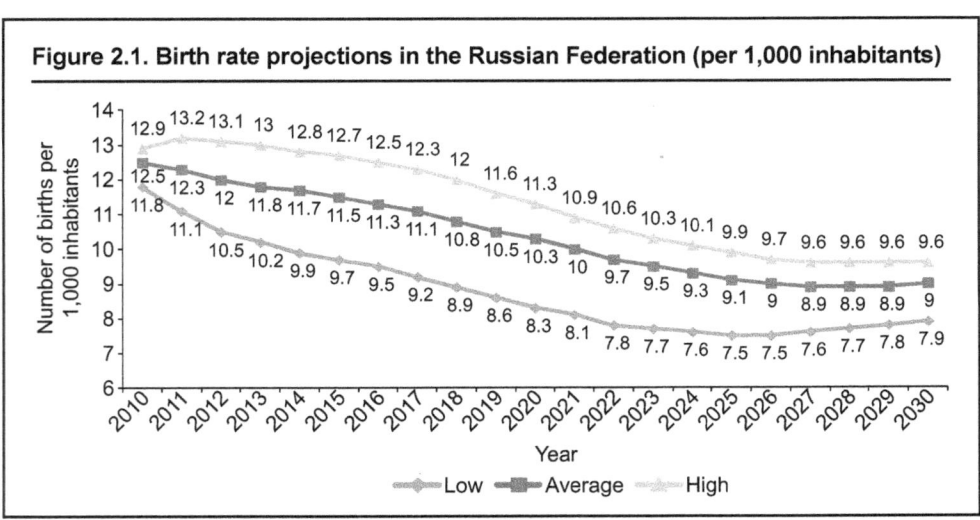

Source: Federal Service for State Statistics of the Russian Federation.

A breakdown of preschool education coverage by type of settlement reveals two important points. First, the situation is continuously more favorable in urban areas, where enrollment has been almost 30 percent higher than in rural areas since 2000 (figure 2.2). Second, enrollment substantially varies among Russian regions: from 86 percent in the North-East (Chukotka Autonomous Region) to 8.8 percent (2009) in the South-West (Ingush Republic).[2]

The changes in preschool enrollment are in line with the broader demographic trends in Russia (figure 2.3), mainly the rise in the birth rate recorded in Russia since the end of the 1990s.

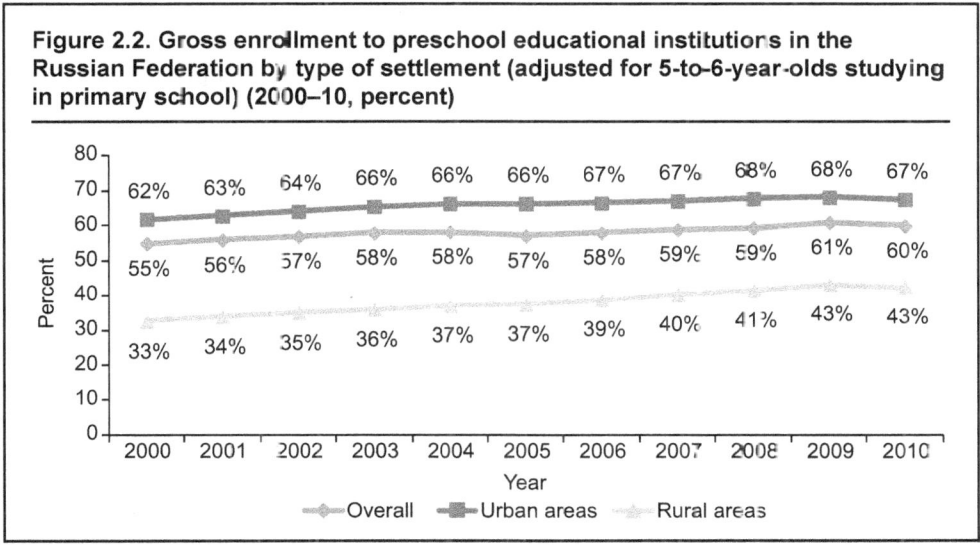

Figure 2.2. Gross enrollment to preschool educational institutions in the Russian Federation by type of settlement (adjusted for 5-to-6-year-olds studying in primary school) (2000–10, percent)

Sources: Data for 2000–08: Abdrahmanova et al. (2010). Data for 2009–10: authors' calculations based on data of the Federal Service for State Statistics of the Russian Federation.

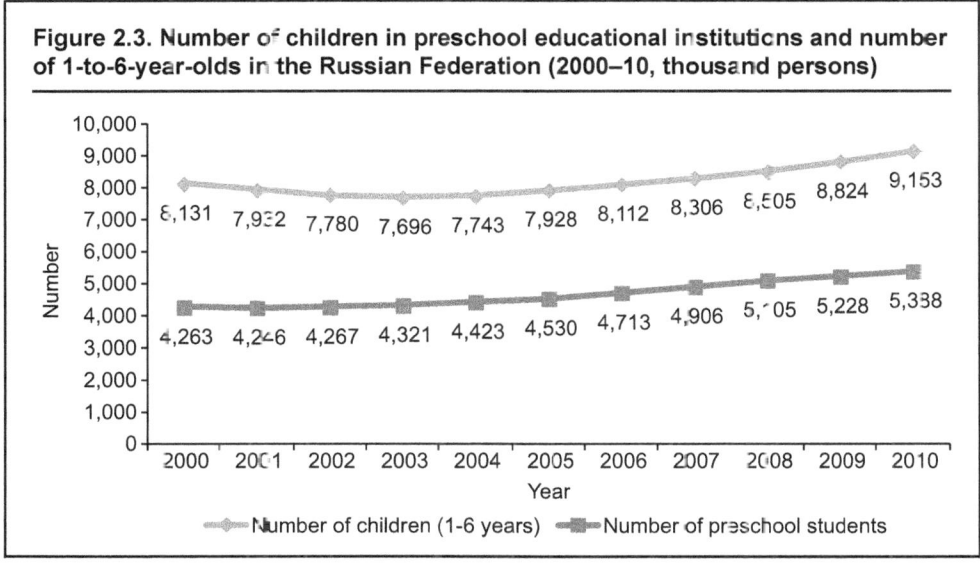

Figure 2.3. Number of children in preschool educational institutions and number of 1-to-6-year-olds in the Russian Federation (2000–10, thousand persons)

Sources: Data for 2000–08: Abdrahmanova et al. (2010). Data for 2009–10: authors' calculations based on data of the Federal Service for State Statistics of the Russian Federation.

By international comparison, preschool enrollment in Russia falls between the rates for developed and developing countries, with 59 percent net enrollment of boys and girls 3–5 years old. The average enrolment rate for children 3–4-years old is 80 percent for the EU19 but only 57 percent for OECD countries not in the European Union (OECD 2010).

Institutional Structure and Scale

The number of preschool educational institutions has decreased in the period 2000–09 by 17 percent in rural areas and 5 percent in urban areas (with overall decrease of 10 percent). Small institutions were either closed or consolidated (figure 2.4).

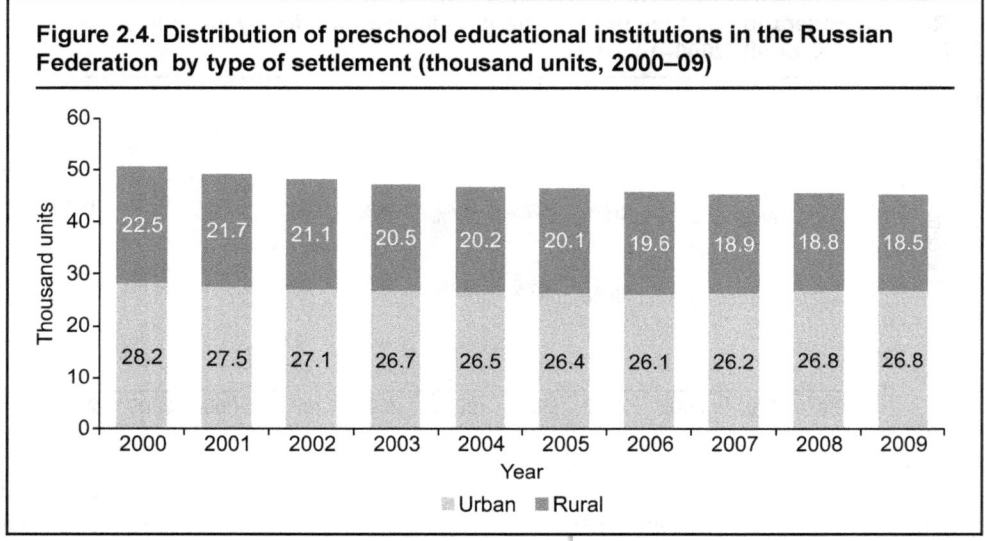

Figure 2.4. Distribution of preschool educational institutions in the Russian Federation by type of settlement (thousand units, 2000–09)

Sources: Data for 2000–08: Abdrahmanova et al. (2010). Data for 2009: Federal Service for State Statistics of the Russian Federation.

Cadres

The qualification requirements to staff employed in preschool education in Russia are lower than in developed countries. The vocational degree is enough to start and continue a career as a kindergarten teacher. Several studies in regions show that there is a significant share (30–60 percent, varying by region) of teachers with higher education degrees. In terms of gender the preschool system in Russia is the most feminized; in many cases there are few or no men in teaching. Most of employed men have servicing professions. There is also no specific policy to attract more men in the system. Hence, there is a certain need to develop new policies aimed at increasing the qualification of ECD teaching staff and caregivers as well as attracting more men in this profession.

Despite the decrease in the number of educational institutions, there has been a significant increase in the number of staff in preschool establishments. Most of this rise is due to a significant increase in nonteaching staff (figure 2.5), which has slightly decreased the student-teacher ratio (students to all staff), and has slightly increased the student-teaching staff ratio (figure 2.6).

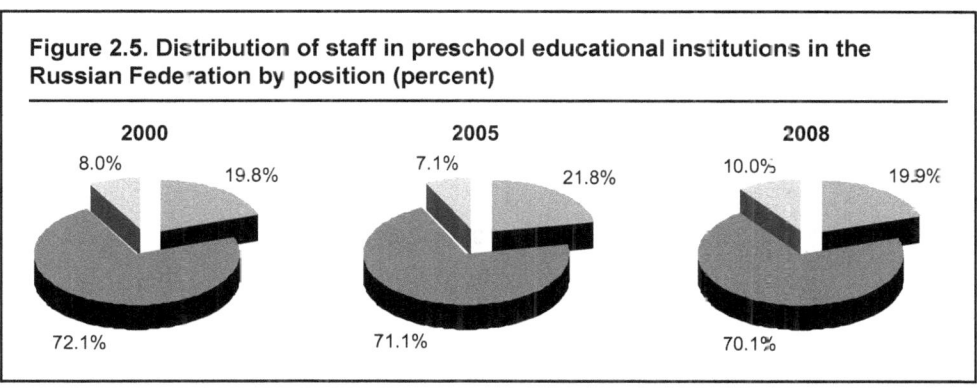

Figure 2.5. Distribution of staff in preschool educational institutions in the Russian Federation by position (percent)

Source: Authors' calculations based on data of the Federal Service for State Statistics of the Russian Federation.

The student-to-teacher ratio in preschool educational institutions was 8.9 in 2010 in Russia, which is significantly below OECD and EU19 average (14.9 and 13.9, respectively) (OECD 2010). Given this consideration, one may alert Russia's authorities that low student-teacher ratio may negatively affect efficiency and quality of services in ECD.

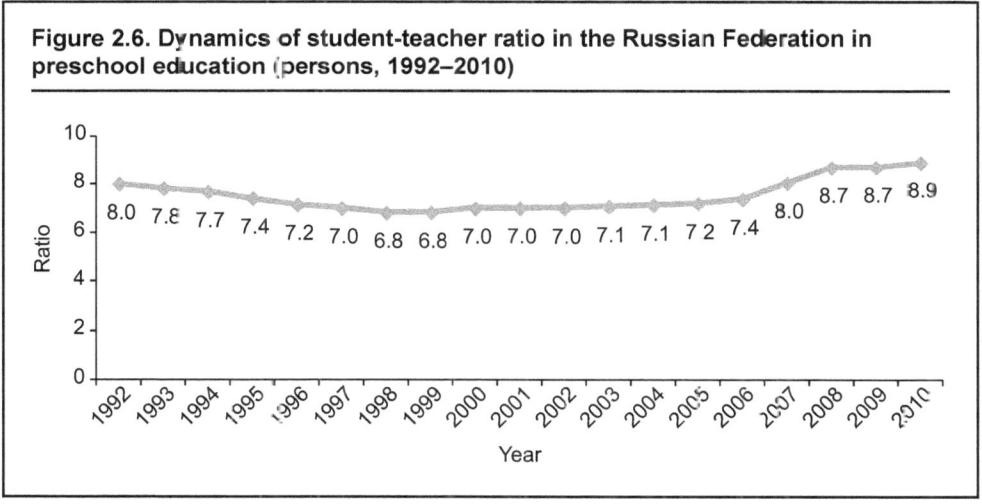

Figure 2.6. Dynamics of student-teacher ratio in the Russian Federation in preschool education (persons, 1992–2010)

Source: Authors' calculations based on data of the Federal Service for State Statistics of the Russian Federation.
Note: Figure shows ratio of students to teachers in full time equivalent.

Financing

The volume of government spending has significantly increased over the past 6 years, growing almost four times from RUR 72 billion in 2003 to RUR 287 billion in 2009. This translates into an average annual increase of 26 percent. However, in fixed 2003 prices the increase in preschool financing has been significantly smaller, growing about twofold during that period. See figure 2.7 from the OECD Family Database, which shows the level of funding across OECD member countries.

10 A World Bank Study

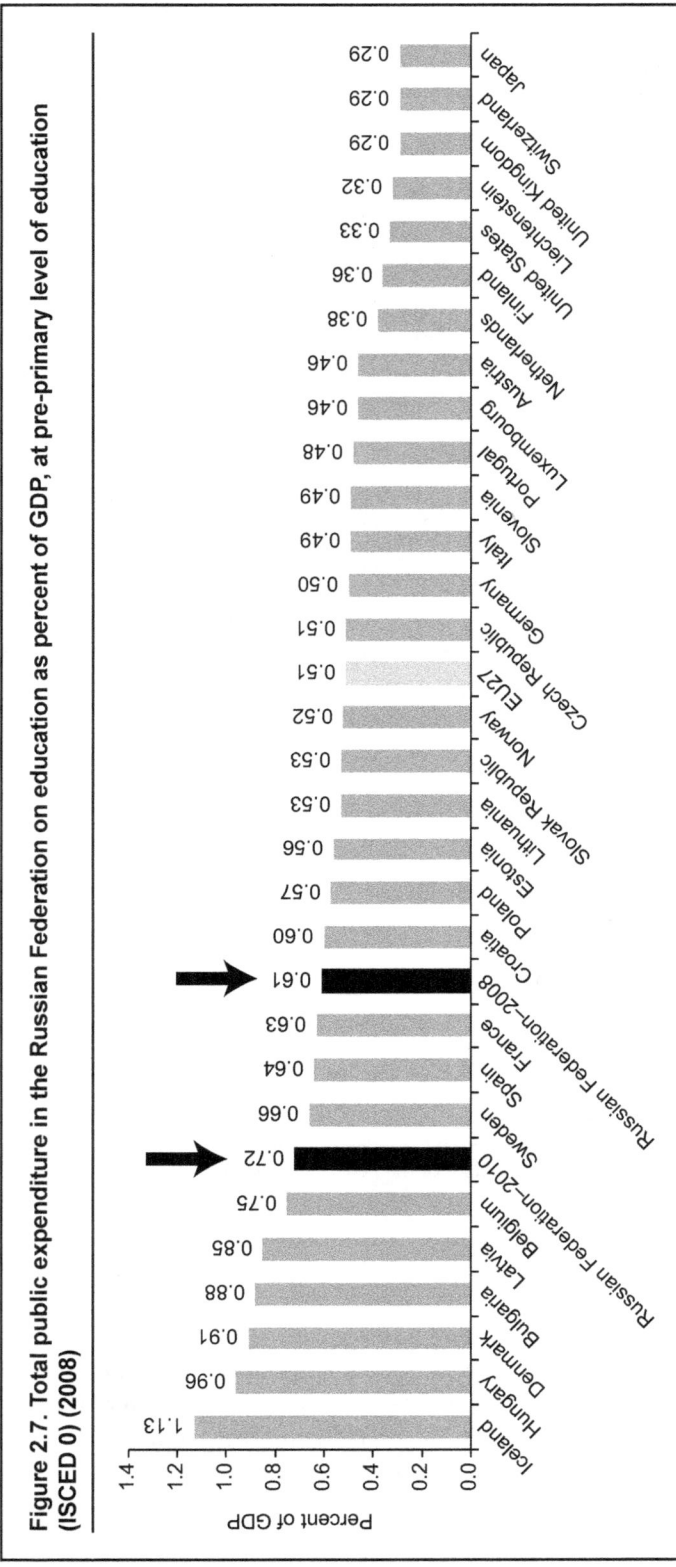

Figure 2.7. Total public expenditure in the Russian Federation on education as percent of GDP, at pre-primary level of education (ISCED 0) (2008)

Sources: Data for Russia: authors' calculations based on data of the Treasury of the Russian Federation, and Federal Service for State Statistics of the Russian Federation. Data for other countries: authors' calculations based on the Eurostat database, http://epp.eurostat.ec.europa.eu/portal/page/portal/eurostat/home/.

In 2008 Russia spent 0.61 percent of GDP on preschool education (ISCED 0), which is higher than EU average (EU27 average was 0.54 percent of GDP in 2008). Evident positive trend in Russia is the increasing share of GDP allocated to preschool education and early childhood development (table 2.1 and figure 2.8). It is worth mentioning that Russia's expenditures on ECD include 6-year-old children, although in many OECD countries these children are already in primary school.

Table 2.1. Public expenditure on ECEC in the Russian Federation, 2003–10

Year	Public expenditure on ECEC in Russia as % of GDP	Public expenditure on ECEC in Russia as % of total state expenditures	Public expenditure on ECEC in Russia as % of public expenditures on education
2003	0.54	1.82	15.16
2004	0.54	1.96	15.45
2005	0.52	1.66	14.09
2006	0.54	1.74	14.02
2007	0.57	1.67	14.12
2008	0.61	1.80	15.30
2009	0.74	1.81	16.15
2010	0.72	1.86	16.97

Source: Federal Service for State Statistics of the Russian Federation.

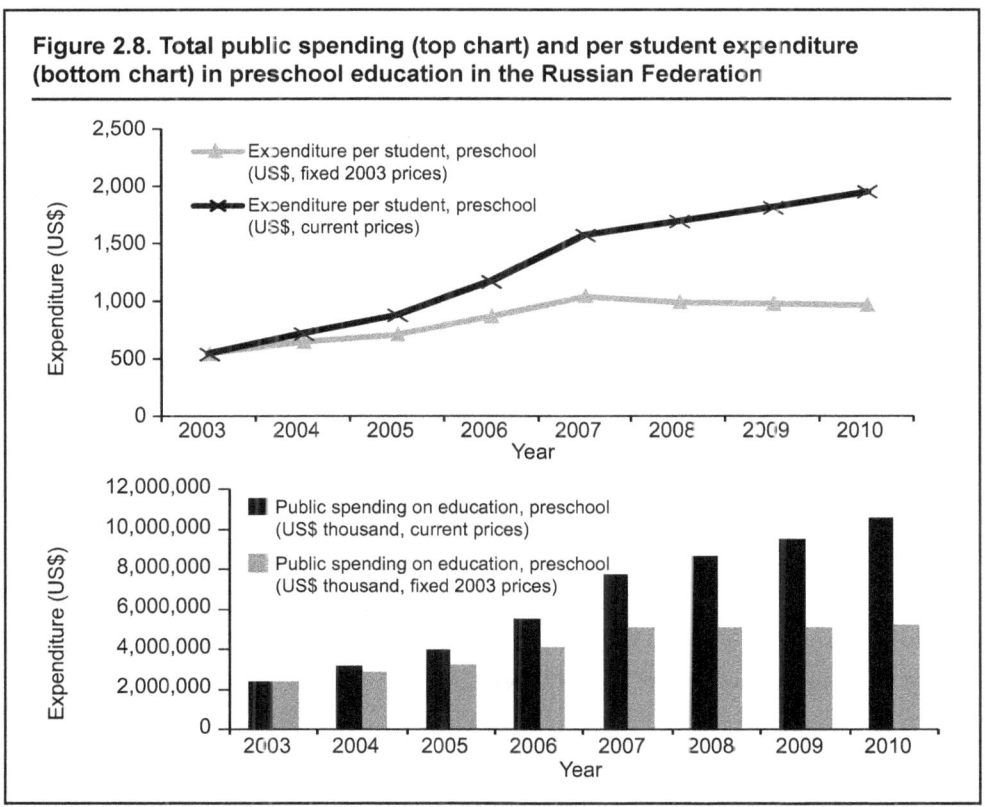

Figure 2.8. Total public spending (top chart) and per student expenditure (bottom chart) in preschool education in the Russian Federation

Source: Authors' calculations based on data of the Federal Service for State Statistics, Treasury of the Russian Federation, and the Central Bank of the Russian Federation.

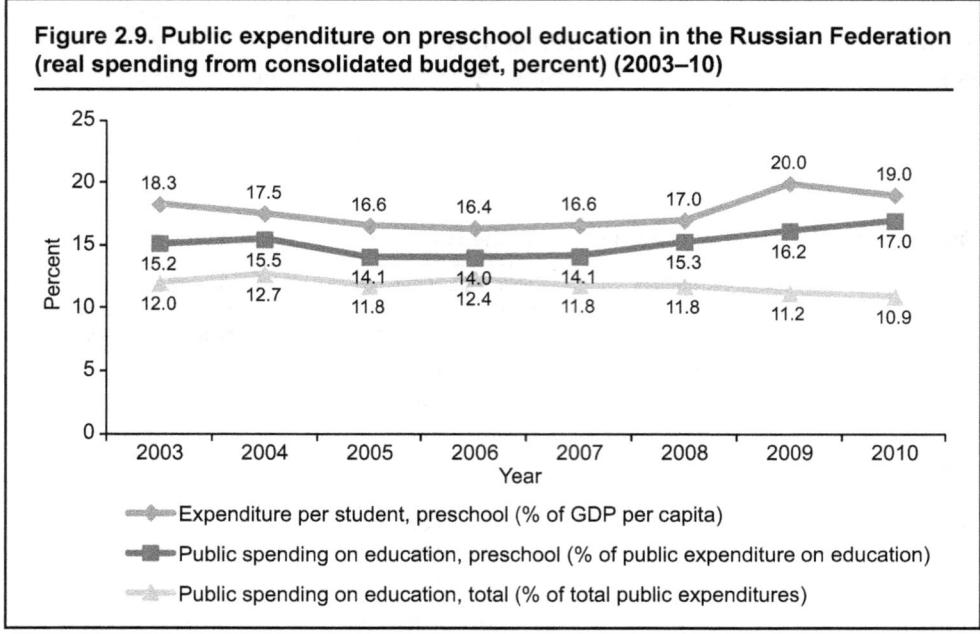

Figure 2.9. Public expenditure on preschool education in the Russian Federation (real spending from consolidated budget, percent) (2003–10)

Source: Authors' calculations based on data of the Federal Service for State Statistics, and Treasury of the Russian Federation.

Per-student investment on preschool educational institutions as a share of GDP per capita has increased by 4 percent points in 2003–09 (figure 2.9). This amount has remained a relatively constant share of government spending on education.

Regional Differentiation

Total regional expenditure on education allocated to the preschool level is generally less than 1 percent of GDP (0.71 percent in 2010). Regions on average spend 24 percent of their gross regional product (GRP)[3] per capita annually on preschool student. In 2009, the rate varied from 2.4 percent in the Center (Tyumen Oblast) to 75.7 percent in the South (Tuva Republic) (see figure 2.10). One common feature typical for almost all Russian regions is the higher enrollment ratio in those with greater amount of GRP allocated to one citizen.

Recent and Ongoing Reforms

Granting of Autonomous Status to Kindergartens

Under the new Russian Budgetary Code issued on January 1, 2009 budgetary institutions (including educational) are granted an opportunity to receive the status of "autonomous institution." Such a step allows administrators of those public establishments to manage resources and to implement their own development strategies.

Kindergartens in Russia have been working on a partially paid basis from the early 1990s. Parents cofinance the programs by paying amounts calculated by the municipalities (basically these payments for care services were not more than 20 percent of the full cost and educational programs are coming at no cost), making kindergartens the first educational institutions that have learned how to operate with off-budget money by

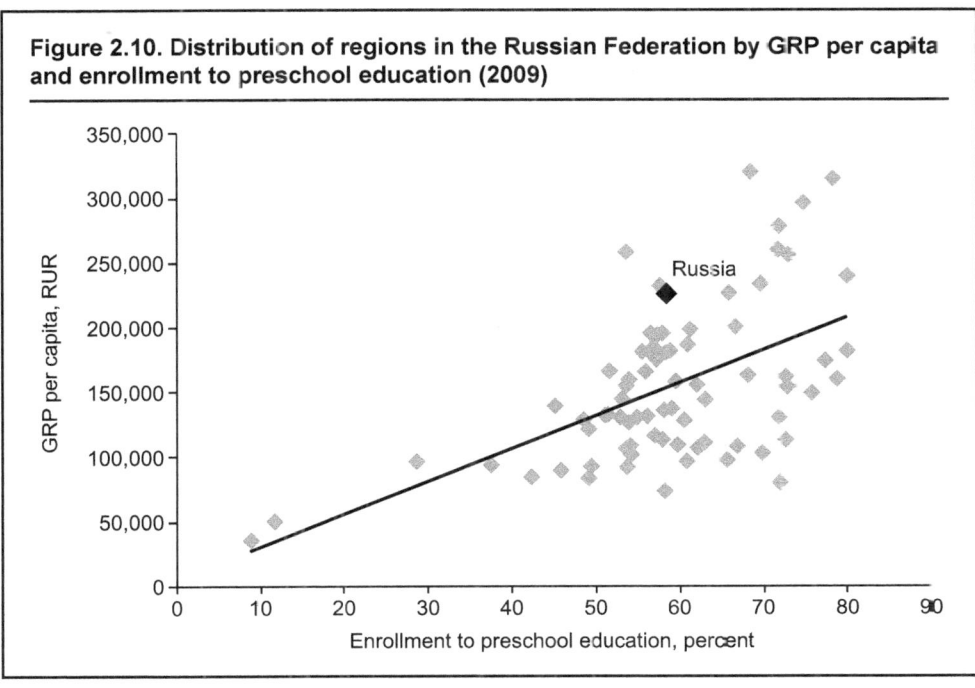

Figure 2.10. Distribution of regions in the Russian Federation by GRP per capita and enrollment to preschool education (2009)

Source: Authors' calculations based on data of the Federal Service for State Statistics, and Treasury of the Russian Federation.

offering various additional paid services. Kindergartens are compact, manageable institutions closely connected with the consumers—that is, families. Because of all these reasons kindergartens more often receive the status of autonomous institution (see table 2.2 and figure 2.11).

Table 2.2. Distribution of autonomous institutions in the Russian Federation by sphere and subordination (data from July 1, 2010)

	Regional subordination	Municipal subordination	Total
Science	16	1	17
Education, including:	274	632	906
primary and secondary schools, nonformal educational centers	137	99	236
Kindergartens	2	533	535
institutions of initial and secondary vocational education	135	—	135
Health	22	6	28
Culture	132	76	208
Social protection	227	6	233
Population employment	34	2	36
Sports	90	60	150
Other spheres	639	120	759
Total	1,434	903	2,337

Source: Ministry of Economic Development of the Russian Federation.

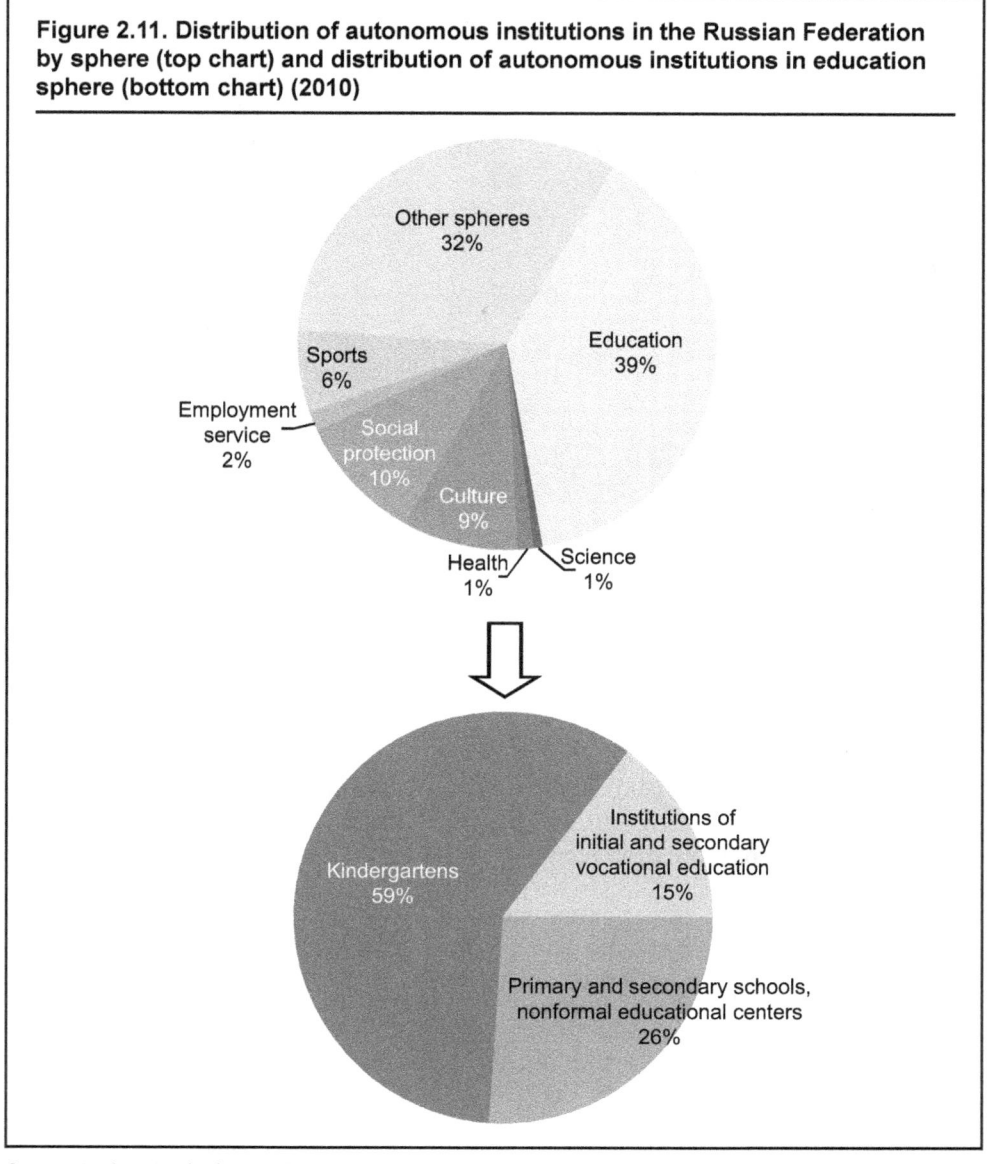

Figure 2.11. Distribution of autonomous institutions in the Russian Federation by sphere (top chart) and distribution of autonomous institutions in education sphere (bottom chart) (2010)

Source: Authors' calculations based on the data of Ministry of Economic Development of the Russian Federation.

Attempts to Solve the Enrollment Problem

In the situation of places shortage in kindergartens, regional authorities have developed several measures to solve the enrollment problem. A good and popular one is restoring of old kindergarten buildings that had been either privatized by entrepreneurs or leased to state organization in the 1990s. Restoring of buildings that are in private ownership is the most complicated process. Beside legal and juridical invasion it requires huge additional financing. In some cases municipal authorities find it cheaper to build a new educational institution than buying it from private organizations.

Buildings that stayed in municipal property are being reassigned back to kindergartens and preschool educational institutions: lease contracts are being terminated and/or annulled. The overall activity is being implemented by municipalities in the framework of programs and financed from regional budgets in the form of targeted transfers (subsidies).

SUBSTITUTION OF SERVICES DELIVERY BY LUMP SUM GRANTS

In some Russian regions (the Perm region for example) compensation schemes have been introduced. These schemes are designed to make money transfers to parents who cannot receive ECD services and are in waiting lists. By giving these compensations to parents regional authorities consider these children as enrolled. Clearly, this scheme is designed to promote the private providers who may receive this money from the families. However, this doesn't guarantee that this money will be purposefully used. It is also known that in disadvantaged backgrounds children are unlikely to receive any services for this money, but they need them more than children from middle class and affluent families. More appropriate arrangement might be based on the educational vouchers that in turn might be used to promote flexibility in the sector of ECD services. The main barrier to this is excessive regulations that do not allow private sector to acquire all required documentation for services provision (including sanitary regulations, requirement to the material environment, fire regulations, and so forth). More flexible approach to regulations including for private provision could enable more provision and increase enrollment.

Permission for Private Providers

Under the new federal law (N 148-FL of July 17, 2009) indemnity payment (compensation) to parents whose children attend nonstate preschool educational institutions and pay tuition fees has been defined. Such changes were made in order to provide equal rights to children in obtaining preschool education; under the Federal Law on Education indemnity payments (compensations) to parents whose children attend state or municipal preschool educational institutions are already provided. With all positive signs of this change, this is only a half measure. The compensation for sustaining costs of the private kindergartens will be paid to only those parents whose children attend full day services at licensed kindergartens. The share of such private kindergartens in Russia is 2 percent. At the same time several anecdotal studies show that up to 8 percent of provision (for example, in Samara city) is delivered by kindergartens that are not registered. Thus, the government needs to take measures to legalize such existing private kindergartens.

Key Problems and Challenges

Access

Early childhood development (ECD), especially for children between the ages of 0 and 3, is underdeveloped in Russia. ECD (0–3) programs that are implemented globally have proved to be the most effective economically and socially. Despite these facts, Russian policy makers fail to realize the importance of early-age programs. There are only a few federal programs specifically aimed at early-age education. Considering the recent demographic changes in Russia discussed above, this lack of federal strategy is troubling.

Russian preschool education shows lower results in terms of enrollment, although it is rather well financed.

Furthermore, almost all Russian regions face significant shortages of places in kindergartens for children between the ages of 4 and 6. The number of required additional places in preschool establishments is growing over time, likewise the demand for services. However, the public system is not that effective in addressing such fluctuations quickly.

Quality

The enrollment rates of early age (0–3 years old[4]) children are decreasing over the years due to high rate of births during recent years (figure 2.12). Thus, there is a serious risk of service quality declining in preschool educational institutions due to overcrowding of

Source: Federal Service for State Statistics of the Russian Federation.

existing preschool establishments. Regions are making efforts to increase the net enrollment of this age cohort in order to keep the situation stable.

Russian authorities strive to protect quality of the services delivery in many aspects. The existing sanitary and construction norms keep the quality and cost of services at a high-level. At the same time the enrollment problem persists. In a situation of budget deficits and low provision of private services the further expansion of public services may slow down. This will be contrariwise with demographic trends.

Policy Options

In developed countries the policy of cofinancing has been frequently supported by following arguments: fewer costs to government, quicker operational readiness, more choices for consumers, better application of energy and innovation of the private sector, better quality due to competition, and so forth. Currently, in Russia, demand for preschool education far outstrips supply (too many children chasing too few places) making it is difficult to see what competition there can be. In reality, the tendency in situations of high demand is for quality to deteriorate, unless there is strong government regulation. Regardless of the validity of these arguments, the reality is that many municipalities are no longer able to fund free, high-quality services, even when helped by the region. How can public authorities bring in private providers in a manner that ensures quality and equity in the sector? The following are policies formulated in OECD countries that achieve high standards while using services supplied by different providers:

- Use, in so far as possible, nonprofit, nongovernmental providers. This is the strategy used widely in continental Europe where some early childhood services are delivered by church groups, humanitarian bodies, and the like. These providers are called "government dependents" as they are not allowed to charge for services any more than public provision. They must also use authorized curricula and are obligated to follow the same regulations as public services. This alliance between civil society and public services can be positive for parents (greater choice) and for the system as whole since nonprofit organizations bring new energy and perspective to governmental practices.
- Impose reasonable registration, licensing, and pedagogical inspections on all services, and encourage accreditation of all services whether public or private—for example, that contact staff working in services should be qualified according to set norms:
  - That recommended group sizes (differentiated according to the age of children) should be strictly respected;
  - That groups should never exceed certain number of children (in case of OECD 18) and should be cared for by at least one qualified pedagogue and qualified child assistant;
- Place a limit on fees charged by providers who receive government subsidies either directly (through per child grants made to the service) or indirectly (through parent fees subsidized, in turn, by government through tax deductions or vouchers).
- Pursue equity in enrollments; that is, to impose an obligation on all services receiving public money to enroll a certain quota of children with special needs or from disadvantaged backgrounds.
- The vision of bringing private partners into early childhood provision is attractive. Private mini-crèches, family day care and child-minders become operational much more quickly than public preschool services, and they can quickly take in children who have been on waiting lists for far too long. However, state and municipal authorities need to regulate such services to ensure that young children and families are treated correctly, and to ensure that the interests of young children are being served. It is not sufficient simply to invite entrepreneurs to deliver early childhood services; the type of service, how it is delivered and its regulation by the state are critical issues.
- Effective preschool education requires establishing high-quality and reasonable standards that have been shown to significantly increase child outcomes.

These include developmentally appropriate, research-based learning standards (foundations), linked to the intentional curriculum, and a comprehensive professional development system, and also culturally and linguistically appropriate curriculum that prepares nonnative language learners for success in school.
- Strict legislation and complicated licensing procedures in the area of construction restrains private sector from construction and sustaining of preschool institutions and slows down the overall process of new kindergartens construction. Thus, in order to improve the situation with enrollment state policy should have focus on less overregulation and more on the educational component.

Notes

1. According to Federal Law on Education.
2. According to data of Federal Service for State Statistics of the Russian Federation.
3. Gross regional product (gross value added at basic prices) is the value of goods and services produced for final use. Gross regional product is calculated by production method as the difference between output and intermediate consumption. Certain types of economic transactions are accounted only for the whole country and included in the calculation of Russia's GDP only. Value added created in the result of multiregional activity does not take into account in calculating GRP. It concerns national defense, government services and other services to the public at large through federal budget. Activities of financial intermediaries, especially banks, which are rarely confined to certain regions, are not taken into account as well.
4. Nurseries and kindergartens in Russia provide care to children at the age of 1+.

References

Abdrahmanova, G., Gohberg, L., Zabaturina, I., Kovaleva, G., Kovaleva, N., Kuznetsova, V., Ozerova, O., Shuvalova, O. 2010. *Education in the Russian Federation: 2010. Annual Statistical Publication*. State University, Higher School of Economics.

Chiganova, S. 2011. "Forming Policy toward Disadvantaged Children." Krasnoyarsk Center for Hippotherapy, Siberian Social Partnership. http://sibsocio.ru/publikacii/71-formirovanie.html.

Organization for Economic Co-operation and Development (OECD). 2010. Education at a Glance 2010: OECD Indicators. http://www.oecd.org/edu/eag2010.

Russian Federation. 2009. Federal Law of the Russian Federation from July 10, 1992 N3266-1 "On Education" (with edits from December 27, 2009).

———. 2010. *Statistical Yearbook of the Russian Federation—2010*. Federal Service for State Statistics of the Russian Federation.

Sitnikova, E. 2011. "Development of New Forms of Preschool Education in Tambov Oblast." Russian journal *"Guidance for Preschool Administrators,"* No. 5.

Voroshilova, I., 2006. "Municipalities Have Nothing to Finance Kindergartens." Russian journal "Amur's Truth," No. 104 (25944).

_____. 2009. http://www.detskii-sad.com/avtonomnie_detskie_sadi.

_____. 2010. "Authorities Expect to Return Back All Kindergartens." http://kidsland.ru/news/3769.html.

CHAPTER 3

Primary and Secondary Education

Current Situation and Trends

Coverage

Primary and secondary education lays the foundation for the development of a broad range of skills and prepares young people to become lifelong learners and productive members of society. Since 1997 Russia has faced a steep fall in the compulsory-school-age population.

The gross coverage ratio for the secondary level of education in Russia is largely in line with the figures for developed countries and shows a high-level of participation of relevant age cohorts (figure 3.1). At the primary level, the country has seen a steady rise in enrollments compared to the United States, Finland, Canada, Norway, and the United Kingdom.[1]

The dropout rate in Russia has been among the lowest in the world. Moreover, the literacy rate has been among the highest in the world reaching almost 100 percent for the past 10 years.[2]

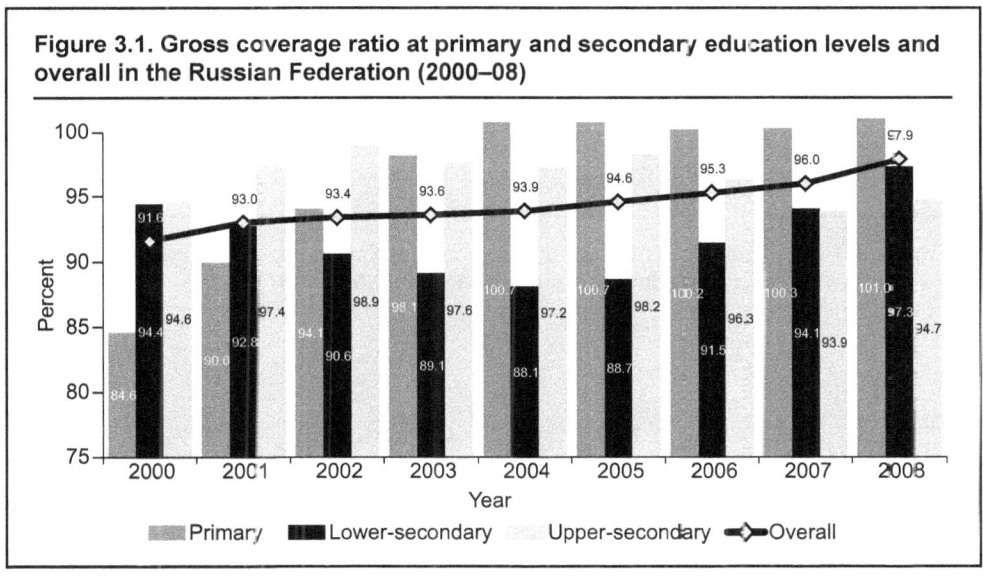

Figure 3.1. Gross coverage ratio at primary and secondary education levels and overall in the Russian Federation (2000–08)

Source: Abdrahmanova et al. 2010.
Notes: The figure defines levels as follows:
Primary education: Ratio of students studying in grades 1–4 to number of 7-to-10-year-olds.
Lower secondary education: Ratio of students studying in grades 5–9 to number of 11-to-15-year-olds.
Upper secondary education: Ratio of students studying in grades 10–11 (12) and students of initial and secondary vocational schools to number of 16-to-17-year-olds.
Overall: Ratio of students studying in grades 1–11 (12) of primary and secondary schools and students mastering upper-secondary education in initial and secondary vocational schools to number of 7-to-17-year-olds.

Institutional Structure and Scale

Facing the problem of the fall in the school-age population, the Russian government has started the program of primary and secondary school optimization. A large number of small schools were either closed or consolidated in recent years. The changes were even more visible in rural areas where the number of schools has decreased by almost 25 percent over the recent decades (figures 3.2 and 3.3).

Another feature of the restructuring process has been the decrease of the number of primary schools. In 2000–10 their number has been cut by 80 percent (figure 3.4). The decrease was not only the result of school closures, but was also due to the process of school consolidation to increase system effectiveness. Often primary schools were merged with bigger schools offering several sublevels of general education.

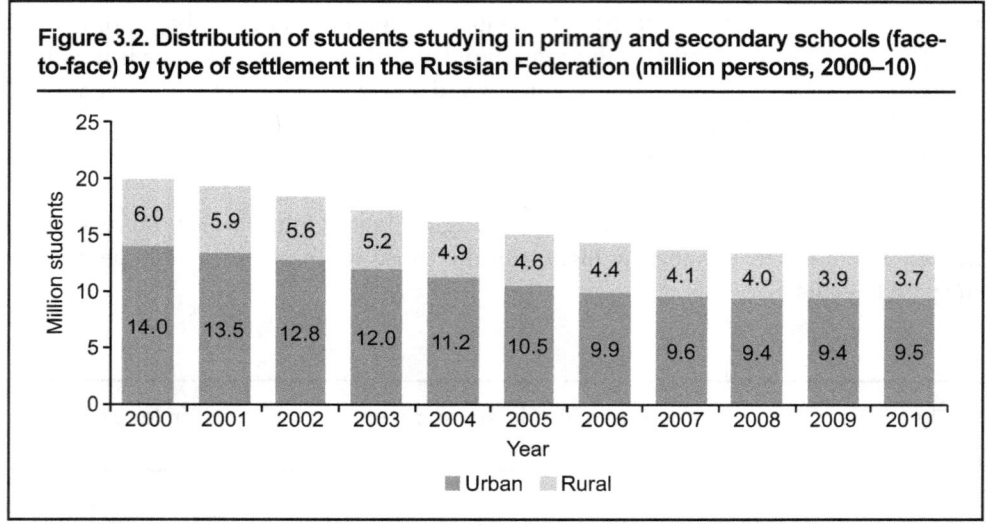

Figure 3.2. Distribution of students studying in primary and secondary schools (face-to-face) by type of settlement in the Russian Federation (million persons, 2000–10)

Source: Federal Service for State Statistics of the Russian Federation.

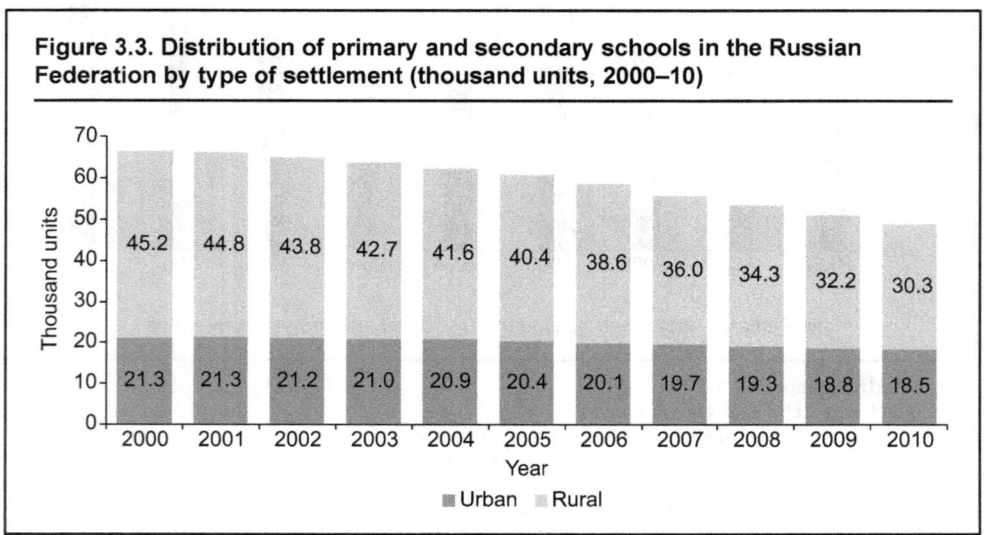

Figure 3.3. Distribution of primary and secondary schools in the Russian Federation by type of settlement (thousand units, 2000–10)

Source: Federal Service for State Statistics of the Russian Federation.

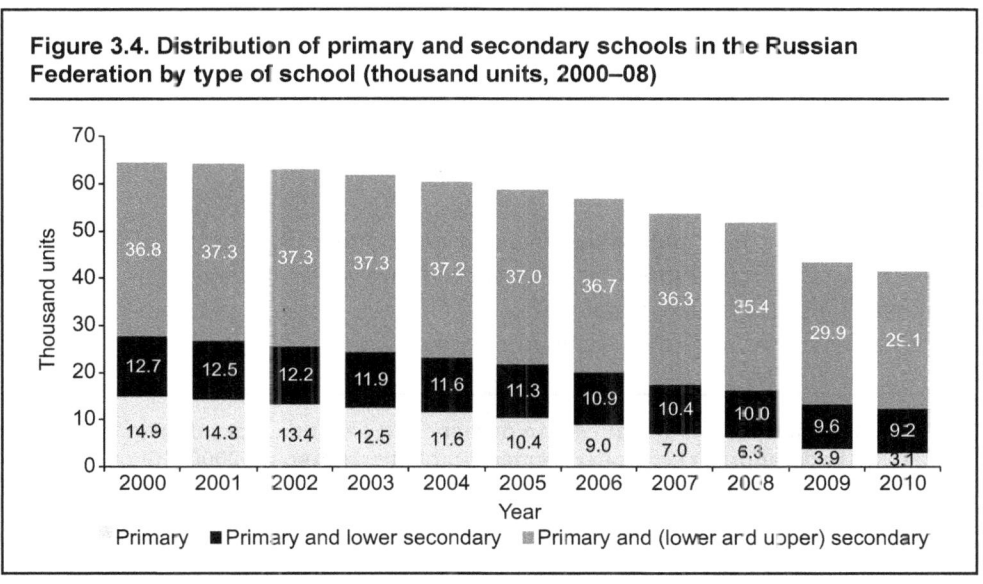

Figure 3.4. Distribution of primary and secondary schools in the Russian Federation by type of school (thousand units, 2000–08)

Source: Federal Service for State Statistics of the Russian Federation.

The impact of school optimization on students was an issue for regional authorities. This process covered not only effectiveness of public funds but also growth of education quality, especially in rural areas. First, the program of school buses was introduced. All the students from distant places started to reach their schools by these special buses. Also some schools started to propose boarding schools in order to accommodate the needs of students.

Against the background of the shrinking school network the number of specialized schools in Russia—lyceums and gymnasiums—has been increasing for almost two decades (figure 3.5). Those schools are provided with better resources both financial

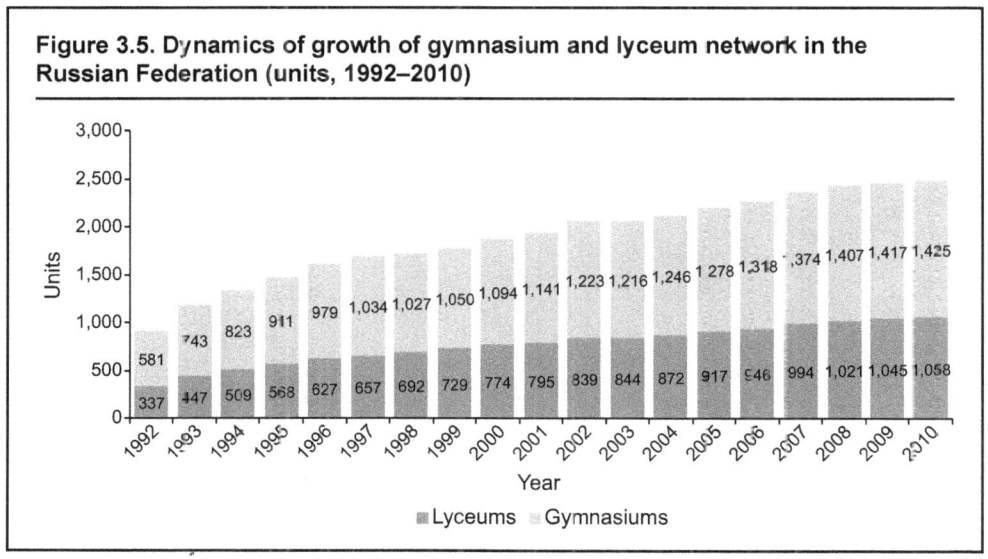

Figure 3.5. Dynamics of growth of gymnasium and lyceum network in the Russian Federation (units, 1992–2010)

Source: Federal Service for State Statistics of the Russian Federation.

and personnel, and thus have better conditions for provision of high-quality educational services. Despite lyceums and gymnasiums comprising approximately 5 percent of the school network in Russia, students studying there represent almost 13 percent of all children in the general education system. Such a trend will lead to the challenge of growing inequality in education system.

Cadres

The size of the teaching staff influences total expenditure on educational institutions through teacher compensation. However expenditure is also dependent on the size of the nonteaching staff in the educational sector. The ratio of teaching to nonteaching staff in Russian schools is 3:2 (2010) (see figures 3.6 and 3.7).

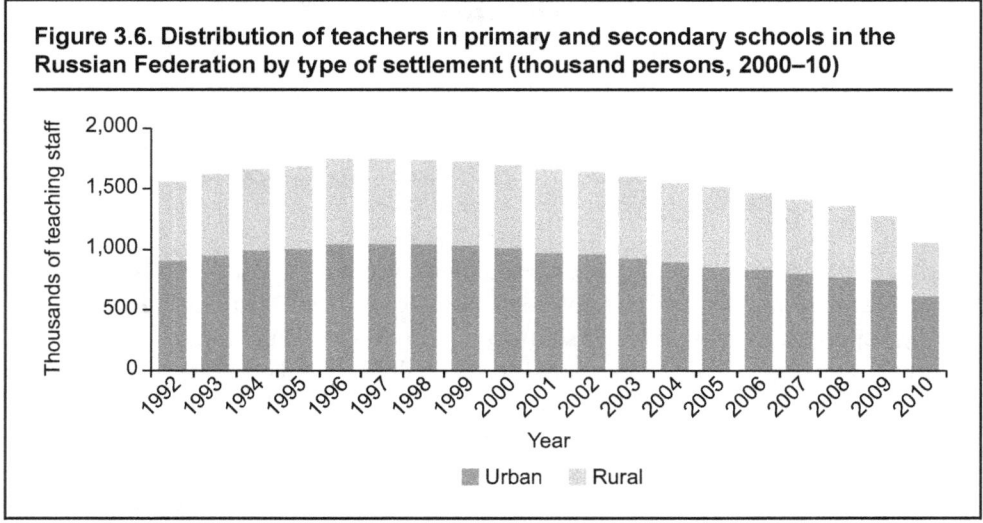

Figure 3.6. Distribution of teachers in primary and secondary schools in the Russian Federation by type of settlement (thousand persons, 2000–10)

Source: Federal Service for State Statistics of the Russian Federation.

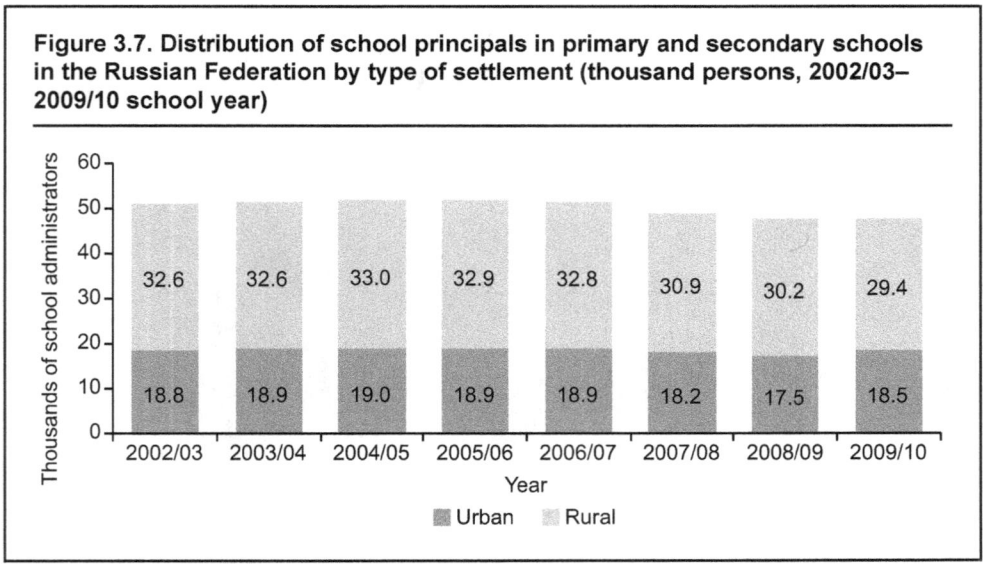

Figure 3.7. Distribution of school principals in primary and secondary schools in the Russian Federation by type of settlement (thousand persons, 2002/03–2009/10 school year)

Source: Authors' calculations based on the data of Statistical Portal *"Statistics of Russian Education."*

Professional experience of teaching in school is one of parameters that influence the level of teacher salary. Thus, the greater the experience, the greater is the teacher's salary. More than half of teachers in Russian schools have professional experience of more than 20 years (figure 3.8). Moreover, almost 20 percent of them have reached pension age (figure 3.9). These factors increase wage funds and overall government financing in education.

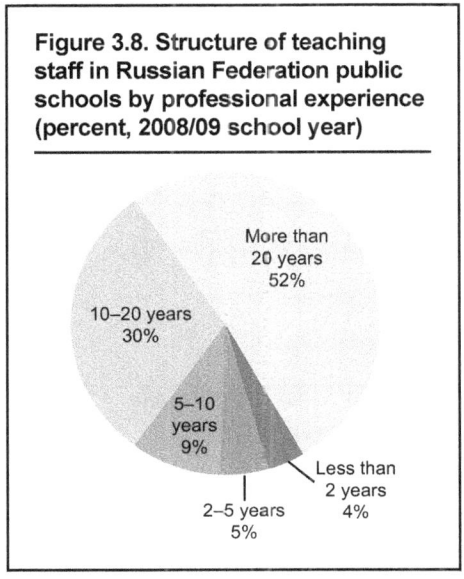

Figure 3.8. Structure of teaching staff in Russian Federation public schools by professional experience (percent, 2008/09 school year)

Source: Authors' calculations based on data of the Federal Service for State Statistics of the Russian Federation.

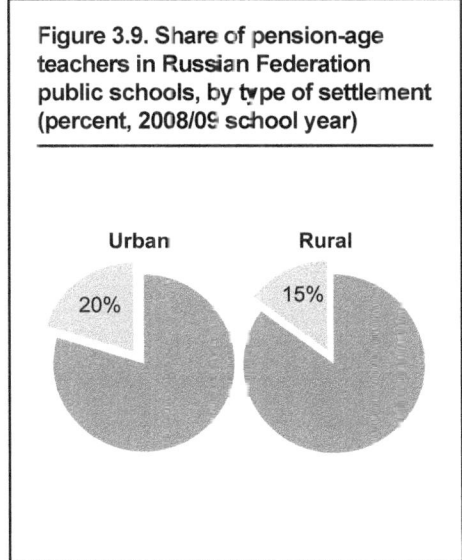

Figure 3.9. Share of pension-age teachers in Russian Federation public schools, by type of settlement (percent, 2008/09 school year)

Source: Authors' calculations based on data of the Federal Service for State Statistics of the Russian Federation.

Distribution of teaching staff by gender shows absolute percentage superiority of females—9 out of 10 teachers working in Russian schools are women (figure 3.10).

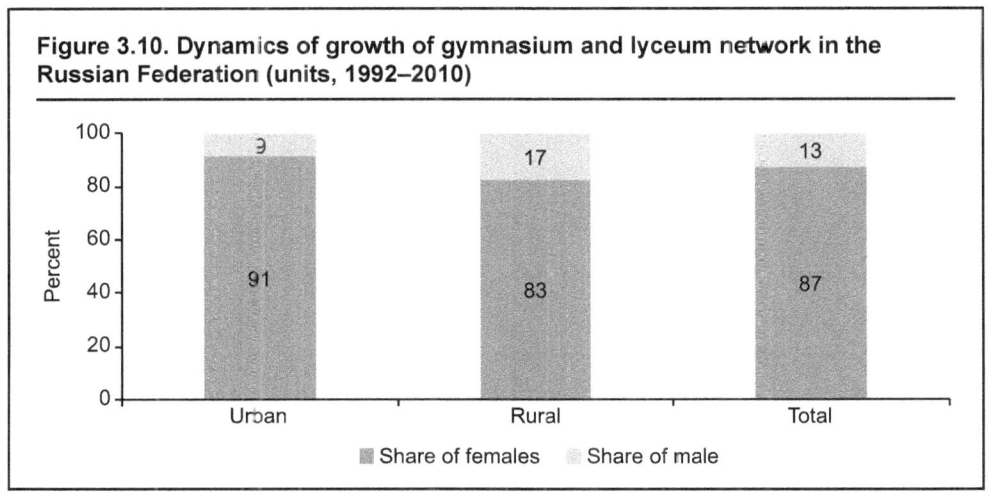

Figure 3.10. Dynamics of growth of gymnasium and lyceum network in the Russian Federation (units, 1992–2010)

Source: Authors' calculations based on data of the Federal Service for State Statistics of the Russian Federation.

The ratio of students to teaching staff in Russia is 17.0 for primary education and 8.8 for secondary level. For OECD countries average student-teacher ratios are 16:1 for primary and 14:1 for secondary education (OECD 2010). Compared to the OECD averages, there is an excess of teachers at the secondary level, which translates into inefficient use of resources (figure 3.11).

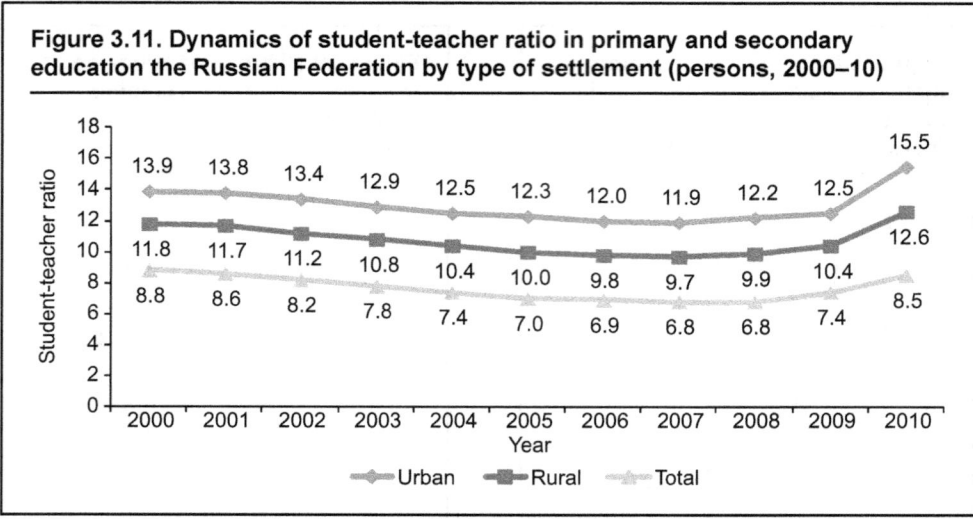

Figure 3.11. Dynamics of student-teacher ratio in primary and secondary education the Russian Federation by type of settlement (persons, 2000–10)

Source: Authors' calculations based on data of the Federal Service for State Statistics of the Russian Federation.
Note: Figure shows ratio of students studying in public primary and secondary schools to number of employed teachers. Calculation of student-teacher ratio for 2009 and 2010 include only teachers in full-time equivalent.

By international comparison average class size is rather small both for primary and lower secondary education (figure 3.12). Under Russian legislation (Medical Norms and Rules), only the maximum class size is set. The minimum class size is not being regu-

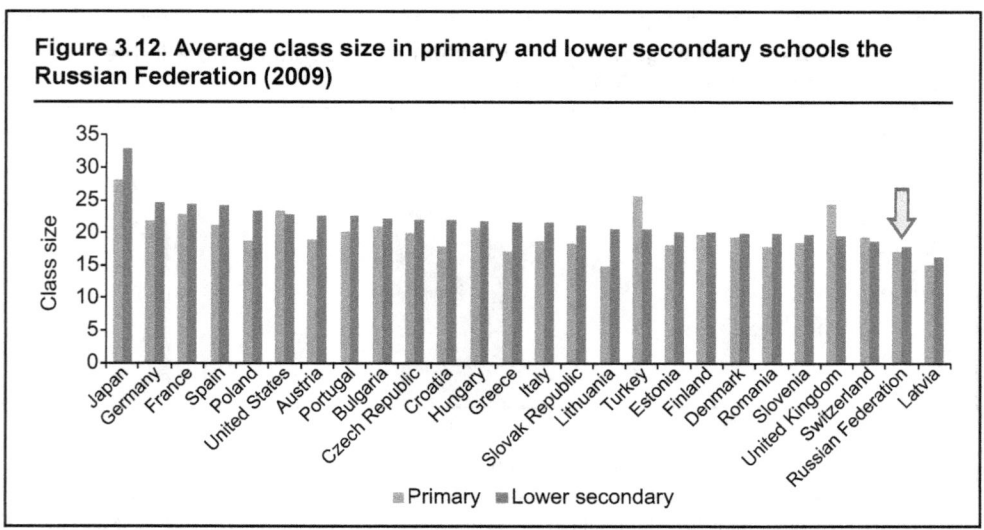

Figure 3.12. Average class size in primary and lower secondary schools the Russian Federation (2009)

Source: Authors' calculations based on the Eurostat database, http://epp.eurostat.ec.europa.eu/portal/page/portal/eurostat/home/.

lated legislatively. All this may lead to overall inefficiency in primary and secondary education system.

Financing

In Russia, more than 75 percent of funds allocated to education are raised and spent at the regional level. Primary and secondary education is totally financed from regional budgets (99 percent in 2010). Russian regions spend annually on average RUR 62,000 (US$2,033) on general school student, although spending across regions varies about 12-fold (2010) (figure 3.13).

The volume of government spending has significantly increased over the past 7 years, growing three-fold from RUR 237 billion (US$7.7 billion) in 2003 to RUR 827 billion (US$27.1 billion) in 2010. This translates into an average annual increase of 20 percent. However, in fixed 2003 year prices general education financing had been increasing till 2007 and afterwards began to decrease.

By international comparison Russia spends less than most of European countries. In primary education OECD average spending is US$6,752 per student and in secondary US$8,346 per student (the EU19 average is US$6,752 and US$8,346, respectively). However, according to its economic development Russian expenditures on secondary education are in line with other countries (figure 3.14).

Disregarding the fall in relative spending on general education represented by its share in total public spending (figure 3.15, top line), per student investments on primary and secondary schools (as a share of GDP per capita) has increased from 15.0 percent in 2003 to 21.8 percent in 2009 and 19.9 percent in 2010.

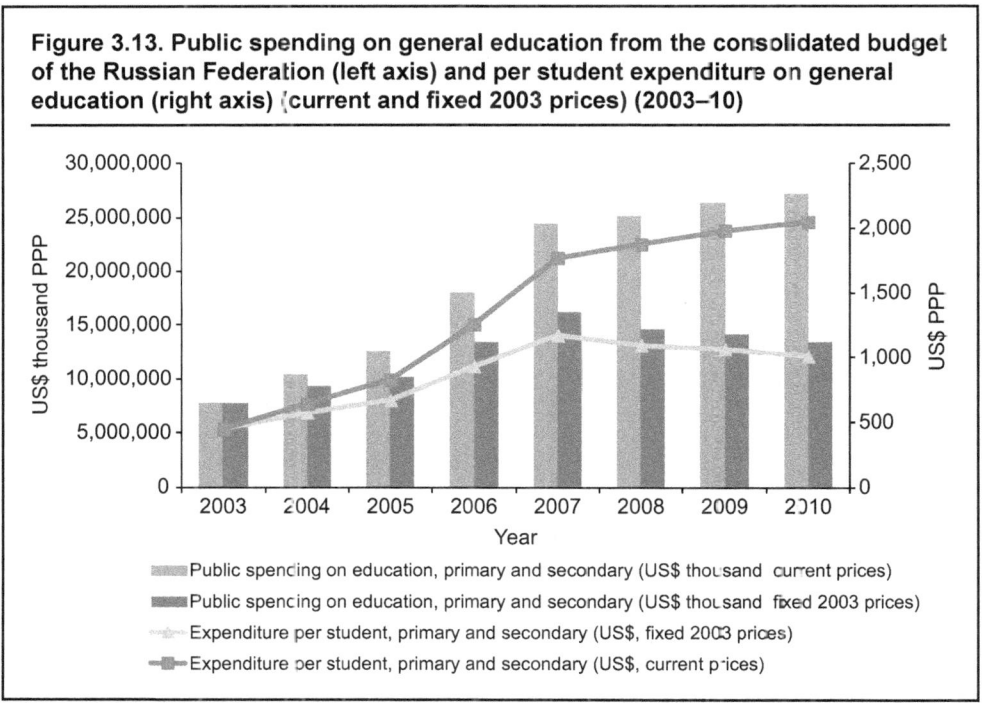

Figure 3.13. Public spending on general education from the consolidated budget of the Russian Federation (left axis) and per student expenditure on general education (right axis) (current and fixed 2003 prices) (2003–10)

Source: Authors' calculations based on data of the Federal Service for State Statistics, Treasury of the Russian Federation, and the Central Bank of the Russian Federation.

26 A World Bank Study

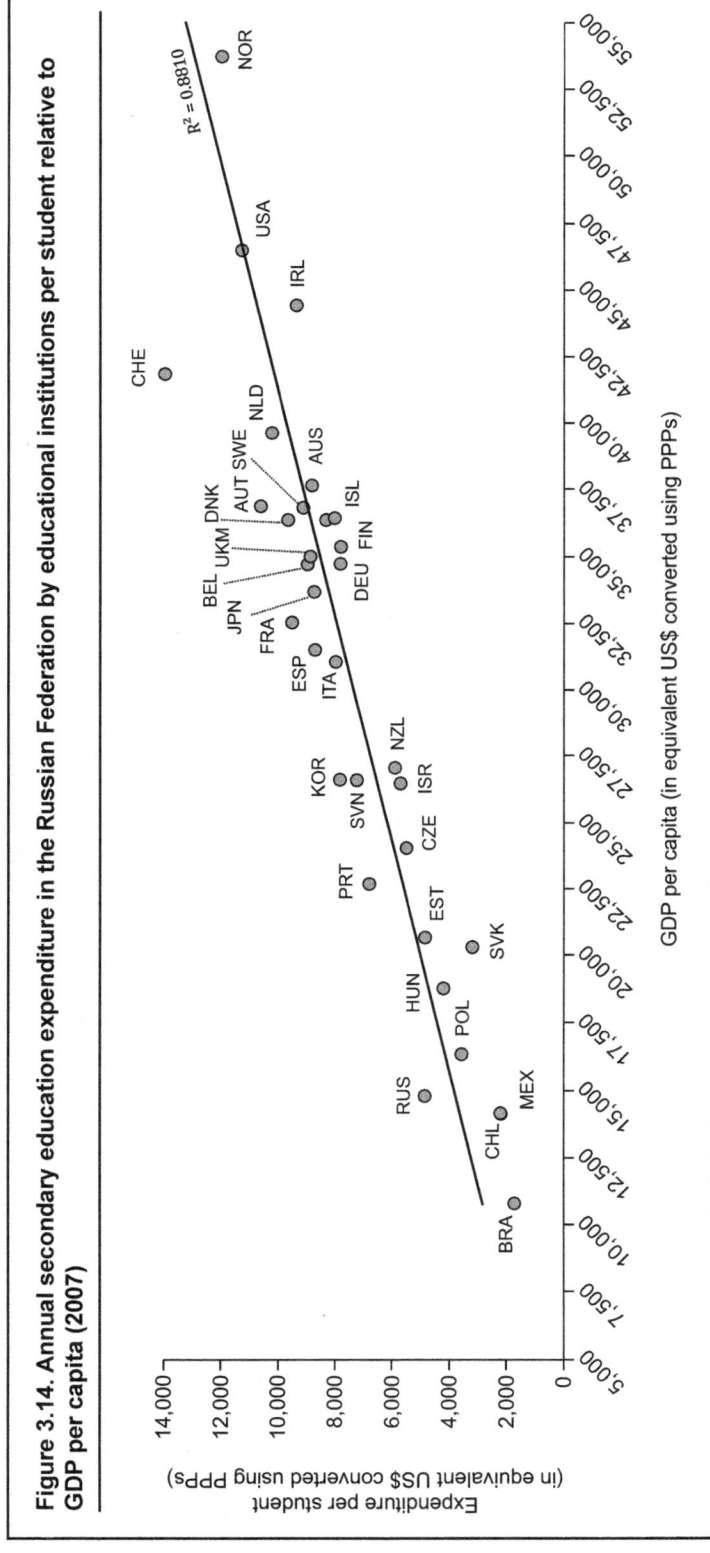

Figure 3.14. Annual secondary education expenditure in the Russian Federation by educational institutions per student relative to GDP per capita (2007)

Source: Authors' calculations based on OECD 2010.
Note: Values are in equivalent U.S. dollars converted using PPPs, secondary education.

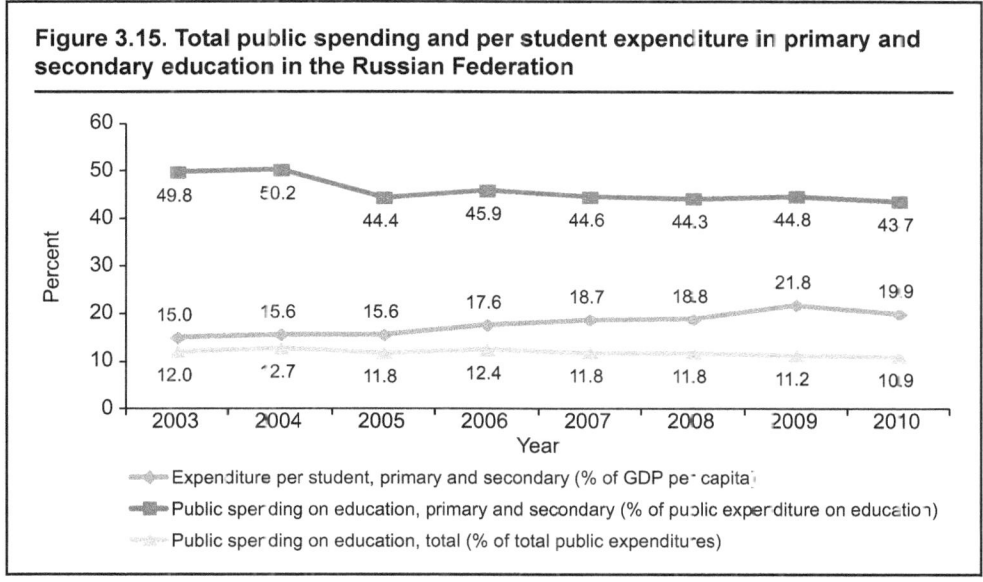

Figure 3.15. Total public spending and per student expenditure in primary and secondary education in the Russian Federation

Source: Authors' calculations based on data of the Federal Service for State Statistics, and Treasury of the Russian Federation.

Regional Differentiation

As said above general education is financed from regional and municipal budgets (about 75 percent of funds come from municipalities and 25 percent from regional budgets). Since the government started implementing the policy of fiscal decentralization, the regions rich in natural resources have been enjoying substantially more funding per student while the less wealthy have suffered chronic shortages.

Data on educational expenditures on general education show wide variations between Russian regions in their levels of total public expenditure as a share of GRP ranging from 0.3 to 13.6 percent (figure 3.16).

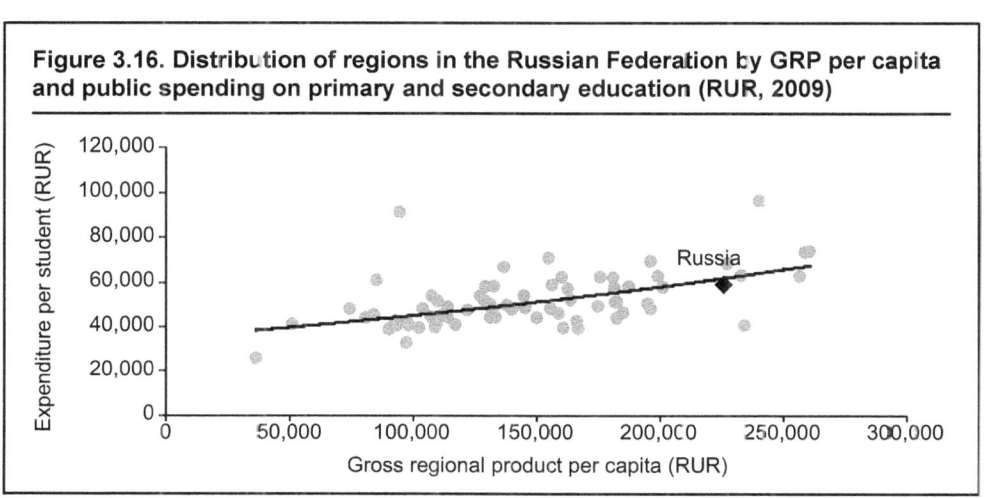

Figure 3.16. Distribution of regions in the Russian Federation by GRP per capita and public spending on primary and secondary education (RUR, 2009)

Source: Authors' calculations based on data of the Federal Service for State Statistics, and Treasury of the Russian Federation.
Note: Chukotka AO, Moscow, Sakhalin, and Tyumen oblast are excluded from the sample as outliers.

Regional variations are exacerbated by the fact that higher-income regions tend to spend more on education from both public and private resources (table 3.1). In particular, regional disparities in funding have led to huge disparities in distribution of material resources for educational institutions across the Russian territorial constituents.

Russia has yet to develop a satisfactory and equitable system of fiscal federalism and service provision, which is particularly urgent for all social services, including education. Increasing federal subsidies to poorer regions and intervening at all levels of power will be instrumental in ironing out regional disparities and ensuring that all schools have enough resources to provide students with basic skills and knowledge.

Table 3.1. Public spending on general education per one student in the regions of the Russian Federation (RUR, current prices) (2002–10)

	2002	2003	2004	2005	2006	2007	2008	2009	2010
Min	4,989	6,474	7,345	8,390	12,077	17,497	18,077	26,021	32,974
Max	76,547	103,477	145,642	177,286	220,282	248,954	297,477	334,680	398,154
Average	11,320	13,383	18,012	22,966	32,919	43,481	54,867	59,125	61,968

Source: Authors' calculations based on data of the Federal Service for State Statistics, and Treasury of the Russian Federation.

Staff expenditure represents the largest cost item. The nominal value of teacher salaries has been on the upward trend since 2000. However, in real terms teacher salaries have been eroding under inflationary pressures (figure 3.17). Despite some increases, as of now, teacher salaries are only 78 percent of the estimated average salary in the Russian economy (2009). The value varies across Russian regions (figure 3.18): from 51.9

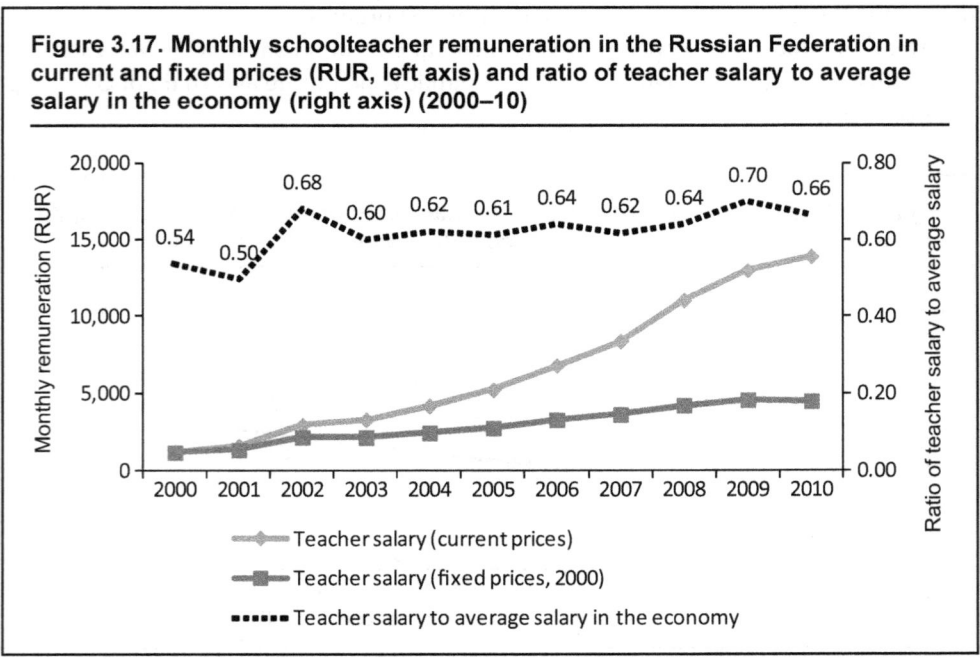

Figure 3.17. Monthly schoolteacher remuneration in the Russian Federation in current and fixed prices (RUR, left axis) and ratio of teacher salary to average salary in the economy (right axis) (2000–10)

Source: Authors' calculations based on data of the Federal Service for State Statistics, and the Central Bank of the Russian Federation.

The Education System in the Russian Federation: Education Brief 2012   29

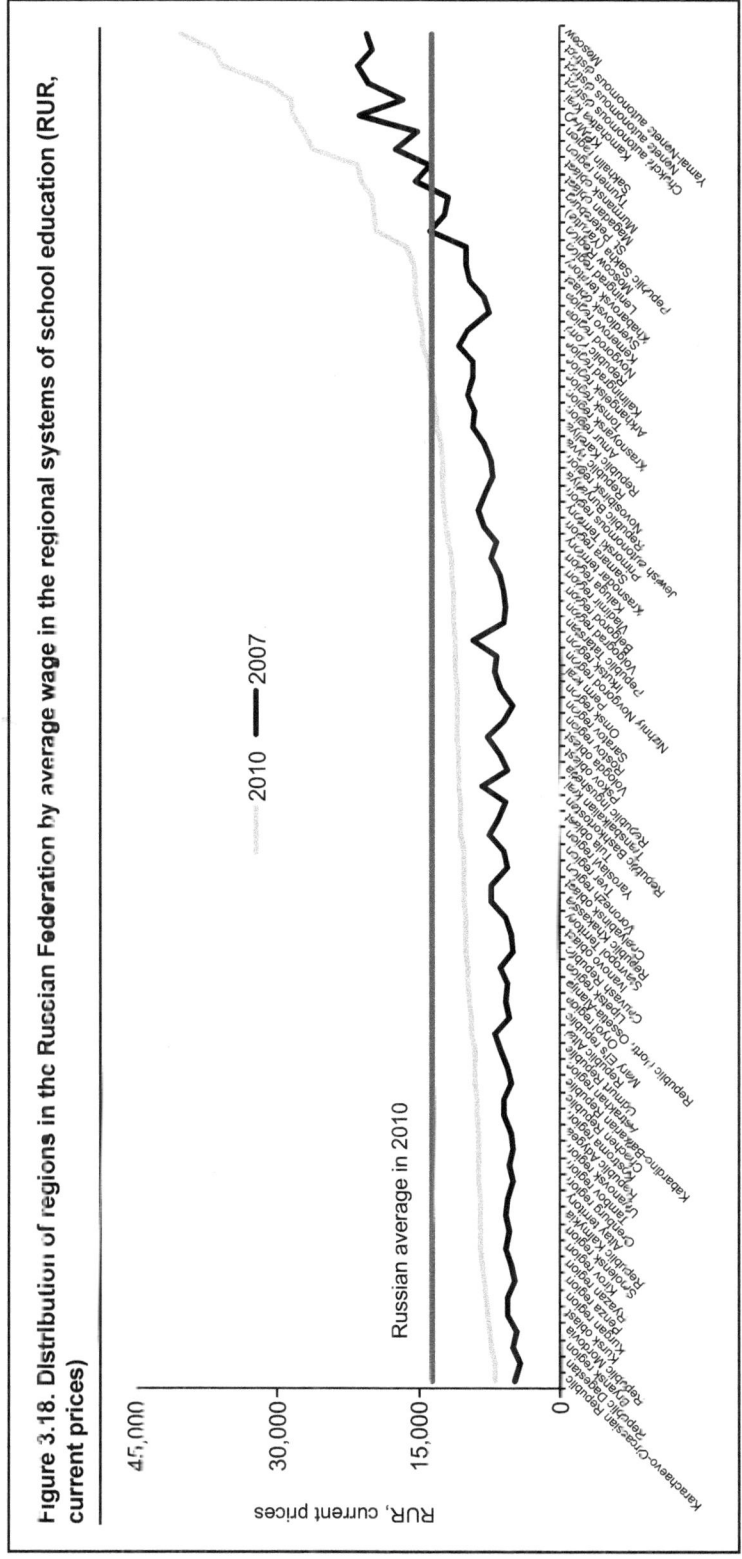

Figure 3.18. Distribution of regions in the Russian Federation by average wage in the regional systems of school education (RUR, current prices)

Source: Authors' calculations based on data of the Federal Service for State Statistics of the Russian Federation.

percent (Yamalo-Nenets AO) to 95.6 percent (Moscow Oblast). Internationally, the ratio of teacher salary to the GDP per capita in Russia is only 0.64 (Agranovich 2005) whereas the OECD average ratio equals 1.23. The data also suggest that teacher salaries are significantly lower than average salaries of other public employees. As of now, there is a lack of recognition of excellence or incentives for performance or training. If this pattern continues, it is likely to jeopardize both the quality and the access to education going forward.

Salary structures are flat and differentiated only by length of experience, status, and workload. Recent research (Soldatova and Kuvshinova 2006) demonstrates salary disparities by status and experience. There is a need to introduce a more flexible mechanism of teacher remuneration that could be tied to teacher performance and depend on concrete outcomes of teacher activities in the classroom. The problem of low teacher salaries and lack of incentives require a long-term solution such as the development of regulatory frameworks and national system of remuneration which will be contingent on the overall funding available for education. Some regions have recently started to move in this direction.

Recent and Ongoing Reforms

Unified State Examination

The Unified State Examination (USE) for school graduation and for university entrance was introduced in 2001 on an experimental basis, and has been rapidly spreading across Russia from an initial 5 regions in 2001 to all 83 regions of Russia in 2009. The Education Reform Project helped bring the best international experience into design of the USE at its initial stage. The USE replaced the existing examination system in May, 2009 when all 83 regions of Russia implemented it on obligatory basis. The USE is designed to protect common standards, decrease corruption and informal payments, and increase access for students from rural areas, low-income families, and the disabled. Enrollments in higher education institutions (HEIs) of the rural population of the relevant age cohort that participated in the USE are growing from year to year. Still the need remains to improve organizational and test content and this could be done incrementally.

Comprehensive Regional Education Modernization Projects

Comprehensive Projects of Education Modernization (CPEM) include performance-based salaries, per capita financing, public accountability, network optimization. The program is one of the most important areas of the National Project "Education." Implementation of the CPEM began in 2007, when the federal center started supporting on a competitive basis efforts of the Russian regions to modernize their educational systems.

These regions have developed the complex projects of education modernization with implementation period within three years, and have taken up certain obligations:

- change the system of labor remuneration, including increasing teacher salaries
- increase the efficiency of budget expenditures by introduction of per capita financing of educational institutions
- create the learning environment corresponding to the modern requirements for secondary education quality improvement, developing a network of educational institutions
- develop and introduce an independent system for monitoring and assessing education quality

- develop public-private system of education management
- develop organizational capacity to realize the project.

Twenty-one regions of Russia received support from the state in 2007–09 within the framework of CPEM. Ten more regions joined the program in 2008, and 10 more regions were selected in 2009.

New Educational Standards

In 2007, work under new generation education standards for primary and secondary school began. The main idea of the new standards was to introduce competence-based standards and establish general requirements to learning outputs and conditions. These included the structure of educational programs, number of hours for studying subjects (to avoid overloading the children), and requirements to key competences, which they should seize.

In 2009 new educational standards for primary education were developed by joint work of educational specialists from the Russian Science Academy, Russian Academy of Education, Russian Academy of Medical Sciences, Moscow State University, Higher School of Economics, Moscow and Saint-Petersburg pedagogic HEIs, and other organizations. The new standards define requirements to educational process, conditions, and outcomes. During 2010 and first half of 2011 all school teachers were to pass courses of professional skills improvement. As of September 1, 2011, teachers have started to instruct all first-grade children under the new standards.

According to the legislation federal state educational standards are to provide (i) unity of Russian educational environment, and (ii) continuity of basic educational programs of primary and secondary, vocational and higher education. Under federal law N 309 of December 1, 2007, the new structure of state educational standards was asserted. New educational standards include three types of requirement including those to (i) the structure of basic educational programs, (ii) conditions of implementation of basic educational programs including cadre, finance, material and technical requirement, (iii) results of educational process. According to the new standards, parents have an opportunity to directly influence the educational process and can be more actively involved in school management, mainly through the creation of school councils. Parents will enter these school councils and create optional courses for their children. This will constitute about 20 percent of all education curricula for primary school. Secondary school pupils together with parents will choose a profile of education and will define optional and additional courses that are necessary for them.

National Educational Initiative "Our New School"

The initiative "Our New School" provides support for gifted children, moral and financial support of teachers, and improvement of school infrastructure. It includes plans to implement the following measures:

- transfer to new educational standards
- development of system for support of gifted children
- development of systems of moral and financial support of teachers
- teacher training and qualification improvement
- improvement of school infrastructure
- development of system for children health improvement

- increased school autonomy.

Development of system for support of gifted children. Russia is going to build an extensive system for identification and support of gifted children. A creative environment to identify gifted children in each secondary school will be developed. Upper-secondary school students will be given an opportunity to study in part-time and distance-learning schools that will allow them to receive specialized education regardless of their residence. To support gifted children various field activities will be organized, including summer and winter schools, conferences, seminars, and so forth.

Systems of moral and financial support for teachers are to be created in Russia. The system of *moral support* is to include already established competitions for teachers ("Teacher of the Year," "I give my heart for children," and so forth). These effective mechanisms for support of best teachers were developed in the framework of the priority national project "Education" and will be further spread at regional level. The system of *financial support* will include not only a further increase of school salary funds, but also create a labor remuneration mechanism that would stimulate best teachers regardless of their professional experience in order to attract young teachers to school. Introduction of new performance-based systems of labor remuneration is to be completed in all regions of Russia in 2010–13.

Teacher training and qualification improvement are also in the focus of the reform. Certification of teachers and administrative personnel is planned to be implemented through periodic validation of teacher qualifications in conformity with the challenges faced by the school. Teacher education will be upgraded and teacher training colleges will be gradually transformed into major basic training centers for teachers or faculty in classical universities.

Qualification improvement programs for teachers and school administrators will be flexibly changed depending on teacher interests, and thus, depending on the educational needs of children. Financing of training will be provided to school communities on the principle of per capita funding. This way, teachers will be able to choose educational program and institutions (not only training institutions, but also, for example, pedagogic, classical universities) by themselves.

Improvement of school infrastructure. In order to establish a universal barrier-free environment to ensure full integration of disabled children in each educational institution, there are plans to update standards for design and construction of school buildings and facilities, sanitary rules and catering norms, requirements for organization of health care to students, and to ensure school safety. In rural schools effective mechanisms for transportation of students, including requirements for school buses, are to be worked out in the 2010–13 period.

Granting of Autonomous Status to Public Schools

Very strong schools can become autonomous educational institutions. Among schools that have already transferred into autonomous status, lyceums and gymnasiums are prevalent. These are school leaders that have additional educational programs and actively cooperate with parents. They have strong governing boards and have introduced their own systems of salaries that stimulate program distribution. They are not always city schools: in some regions even rural schools have passed to autonomous status. But they are united by the fact that they are strong institutions with their own development programs and funds that they would like to keep.

As always, there are problems in some regions where regional authorities are transferring all schools into autonomous status (see figure 3.19). For them this is a process of budget cost optimization, not of network development. In such cases weak schools are at times hurt because they are not ready to work independently.

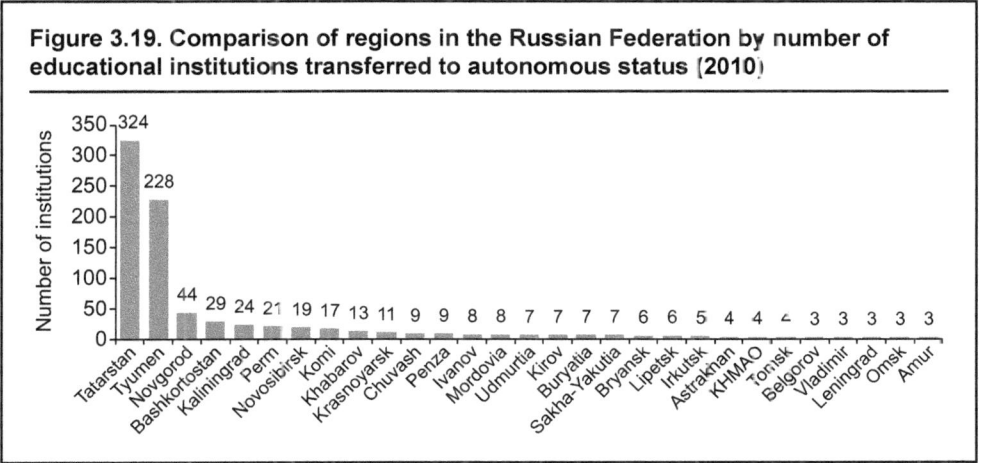

Figure 3.19. Comparison of regions in the Russian Federation by number of educational institutions transferred to autonomous status (2010)

Source: Ministry of Economic Development of the Russian Federation.

Key Problems and Challenges

Access and Equity

Regional inequalities in educational funding pose a threat to access, as decentralization in Russia has led to rising inequality in the availability of funds among local education authorities. Rural regions are especially likely to suffer as a result, as they are often poorer and have little access to high-quality education.

The situation with inequalities in provision of resources to schools is alarming. Government policy of supporting best-performing schools has led to widening of the gap between poor-performing and well-performing schools. The gap concerns inputs (financial and cadre resources provided to schools), as well as outcomes (test results). Policy makers try to attribute low results of poor-performing schools to the disadvantaged backgrounds of students studying in such schools (including problem children, migrants, children of large families, and so forth). Those schools are not being supported by the government and find themselves isolated from the real world. According to results of the recent study (Frouminet al. 2011) students in such schools don't/rarely participate in interschool contests, conduct research activities, and as a result show low test scores.

Quality

International comparison. Russian participation in international studies (such as the OECD Programme for International Student Assessment—PISA) provides a certain understanding of the level of quality of education in Russia in comparison with other countries. The data of the PISA study show that the results of 15-year-old Russian students are significantly lower than both the students' results in leading countries and average results by students of the 30 OECD countries (Agranovich and Korolyova 2006).

International education studies like PISA show the real performance of education system comparing to other countries. Russia participated in PISA in 2000, 2003, 2006, and 2009. The PISA results were an unpleasant surprise for Russia as it systematically placed poorly: 37–40 places (out of 65 countries) in science performance, 41–43 in reading, and 38–40 in mathematical performance. Looking at the absolute score of Russian students, it can be said that the overall level of Russian performance in PISA wasn't stable (figure 3.20). Nevertheless, between 2000 and 2009 performance of Russian students worsened both in reading and math.

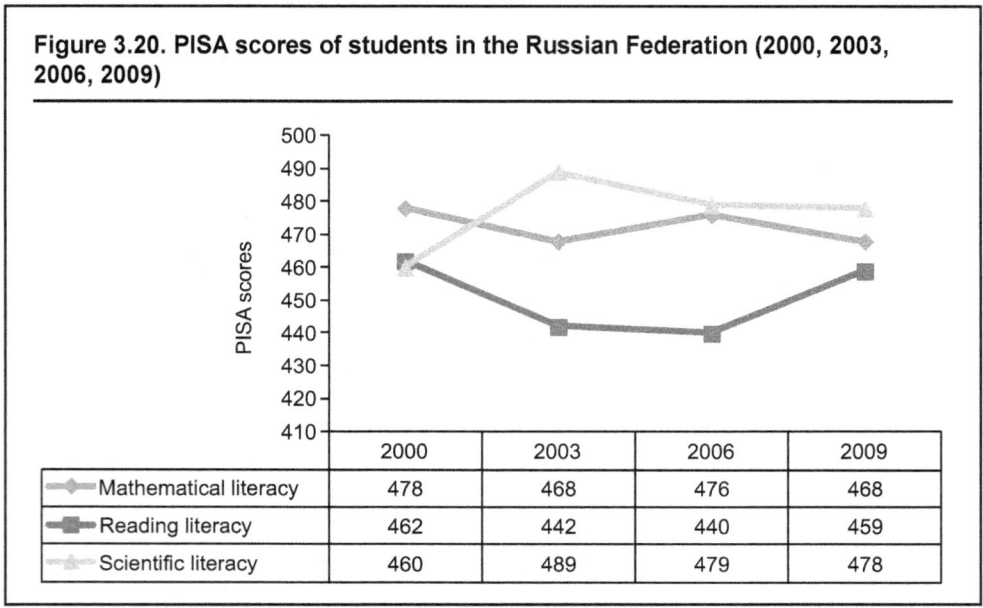

Figure 3.20. PISA scores of students in the Russian Federation (2000, 2003, 2006, 2009)

	2000	2003	2006	2009
Mathematical literacy	478	468	476	468
Reading literacy	462	442	440	459
Scientific literacy	460	489	479	478

Source: Authors' calculations based on the data of "PISA-2009 Key Findings."

Nevertheless, Russia has showed significant progress between PIRLS 2000 and 2006 testing. In 2000 Russia placed 12th out of 37 countries; in 2006 Russian primary school students showed the best results among 40 countries that participated.

The Trends in International Mathematics and Science Study (TIMSS) provided reliable and timely data on the mathematics and science achievement of Russian students. In 2007 Russia showed 10th place out of 59 countries. In mathematics Russian fourth-grade students placed 6th among 36 countries (for example, after Hong Kong SAR, China; Singapore; Taiwan, China; and Japan). Russian eight-grade students placed 8th out of 49 (for example, after the four countries listed above and the Republic of Korea). In natural science Russian primary school students placed 5th out of 36 (for example, after Singapore and Taiwan, China); secondary school students placed 10th out of 49 countries (for example, after Singapore; Taiwan, China; Japan; Korea; the United Kingdom; and the Czech Republic).

Results for the given investigation (of PISA) acquired in the years 2000–09 demonstrated that for all key indicators of functional competence Russian students graduating from basic school essentially fell behind from their counterparts in most developed countries. Ability to reproduce knowledge and apply known algorithms dominate in the profile of achievements of Russian students in comparison with the high-level intellectual skills (generalization, analysis, forecasting, generation of hypothesis, and so forth).

Russian students tend to develop theoretical knowledge rather than practical skills. The standards of teacher training are very rigid and do not contain enough classroom practice when compared with many other countries. It is a common practice for the teachers to ascribe student failures to low student abilities and not to outdated teaching and learning practices.

The overall low quality of Russian education can also be observed from the results of the USE. The data demonstrate that in 2008 only about 7.2 percent of students scored highest in the math test while 23.1 percent out of all students received an unsatisfactory grade (failed the test), which is quite alarming. However, the share of students failing the test in math decreased first to 6.8 percent in 2009 and then to 5.2 percent in 2010.[3] Nevertheless, the results suggest that the quality of education is largely moderate with over one third of students receiving a good grade on the tests in *all* subjects except foreign languages.

Inefficient use of ICT. There have been significant advances in the spread of information and communication technology (ICT) in Russian education. The number of students per one modern computer improved from about 500 in 2000 to 20 in 2008. During 2009/10 school year this number decreased to 16 students per one computer. In 2007, under the framework of a federal program, all schools were to be provided with a connection to the Internet. However, according to data of Russian Federal Statistics Service only 1 out of 2 computers in schools had a connection to the Internet in 2009/10 school year. Significant resources were spent on the production of digital educational resources and teacher training. However, there is little evidence of changes in educational practices enhanced by ICT.[4] Teachers tend to use ICT to support traditional teaching rather than to move to a constructivist and student-centered model. The World Bank–financed e-Learning Support Project has already helped seven Russian regions introduce ICT into education to change traditional teaching and learning patterns. Recently, many other regions have also included such activity in their educational policy and now implementing ICT in education projects on a regional level.

Russian schools have established reasonable ICT infrastructure. Still, Russia falls behind EU averages for such indicators—there are 9 students per one computer, including 10 students per one PC connected to the Internet. Moreover, according to the Ministry of Education of Russia the ICT potential is not being sufficiently used in regional education systems. Efficient ICT use is limited as the technologies are used exclusively during computer science classes and rarely utilized for other subjects, or beyond classes for individual projects, research, and informal learning.[5] The capacity of ICT to support independent or collaborative learning, development of creativity and research abilities, and interactive activities is insufficiently used.

Financing and Provision of Resources

Despite some increases in human development spending, public expenditure on education has been low in global comparison. As compared to the OECD countries where the average public spending on education equals to 5.4 percent of GDP (4 percent in Russia), education in Russia has a markedly lower financial priority.

Considering human resources, the Russian education system remains labor-intensive compared to other countries. This fact is expressed in the low student-teacher ratio and small average school size.

Persistent problems associated with underfunding of the education system (obsolete hard and soft infrastructure, inadequate resources, undertrained and underpaid teachers, and so forth) are compounded by inadequate and inefficient use of resources. This in turn means that Russia is not always able to direct funding to programs that require special attention and support according to national educational, social, and economic development priorities. The present system of allocations, regulations, and incentives leave little for capital investments and development (as little as 5–6 percent of regional educational budgets goes to capital expenditures and investments). A significant number of schools are in need of capital repair and reconstruction (22.6 percent of schools in 2009/10 school year).

Policy Options

Current ways of modernizing the education system are developed well enough, but the implementation of all plans could be very difficult because of misunderstandings and imitations of reforms on the regional and municipal levels. For example:

- *New generation standards implementation.* There should be a strategic vision of the teacher retraining process. Otherwise, teachers would not change the learning process to fit with the new standards.
- *Per capita financing.* In the majority of Russian regions per capita coefficients were created as a way to make payments equal to previous budget system. This is just an imitation of per capita financing and will not bring any results.
- *New system of teachers' salaries.* Because of financial and economic crisis, many regional education budgets were cut down. A a result, performance bonus on teachers' salaries became very small. This needs to be changed; otherwise, current salaries will not make teachers interested in self-development and learning innovations implementation.
- *Regional disparities.* State policy on the matter of financial support is oriented toward best-performing municipalities, schools, students.[6] In order to smooth regional disparities it is crucial to provide support not only to the best, but also to those lagging behind.
- *ICT in education.* More regions in Russia should implement ICT in education programs. Students and teachers should learn how to effectively use modern ICT in solving educational, professional, and everyday problems. They should learn how to search for the information they need; organize, process, analyze, and evaluate it; and create and distribute information in accordance with their needs. All the above-listed skills should enable students and teachers to:
  - effectively participate in lifelong learning (including distance education via Internet)
  - prepare themselves to future professional activities
  - live and work in an informational society and knowledge economy.

- Emphasize teaching methodology and turn it into a new form of sharing good practices through formal or informal communities of practice, to speed up the needed change in effectively using ICT in teaching and learning.
- Target help for different groups of children. Attention paid to children with disabilities should be the same as to attention to gifted kids. The challenge of including such children (with disabilities) in normal school life should be solved (Simakova 2009).
- Special attention should be given to schools showing low educational results and students studying there. It was found (Froumin et al. 2011] that often such schools have to deal with children from large families, migrants' children, or problem children. Thus, there is a need to develop special measures and provide those schools and children equal opportunities.
- The Russian government has tried to implement some projects to involve young professionals in schools. But all these incentives seem to be unrelated to each other and implemented without a strategic view. These incentives show no results. The problem of teacher competitiveness remains to be solved.

Notes

1. The coverage ratio can be over 100 percent due to the inclusion of overaged and underaged pupils/students because of early or late entrants, and grade repetition.
2. According to data of UNESCO Institute for Statistics.
3. Unified State Examination scores are made on the basis 100-point scale, and were converted to a 5-point scale used in Russia. Thus, it was possible to calculate the share of excellent students and share of poor students. However, in 2009 Ministry of Education and Science of Russia decided not to convert scores to the 5-point scale.
4. According to data from monitoring report of Federal Agency of Education.
5. Ibid.
6. For example, Decree of President of the Russian Federation from 28.06.2007 № 825 "On the Evaluation of the Efficiency of Executive Bodies of Regions of the Russian Federation."

References

Abdrahmanova, G., Gohberg, L., Zabaturina, I., Kovaleva, G., Kovaleva, N., Kuznetsova, V., Ozerova, O., Shuvalova, O. 2010. *Education in the Russian Federation: 2010*. Annual statistical publication. Moscow: State University, Higher School of Economics.

Agranovich, M. 2005. "Russian Education in the Context of International Indicators." Analytical report, Federal Service for State Statistics of the Russian Federation. Moscow.

Agranovich, M., Korolyova, N., et al. 2006. Federal Service for State Statistics of the Russian Federation. "Youth Development Report: Condition of Russian Youth." Retrieved July 21, 2006. http://portal.unesco.org/en/ev.php-URL_ID=31337&URL_DO=DO_TOPIC&URL_SECTION=201.html.

Artem, K. 2009. "Children Under Reform". Russian journal *"Expert-Ural,"* No. 34 (388). http://www.expert-ural.com/25-0-7954/

Federal Agency of Education. 2009. Statistical Monitoring Report of Federal Agency of Education. http://www.ed.gov.ru/.

Federal Service for State Statistics of Russia. 2010. *Statistical Yearbook of the Russian Federation—2010*. Moscow.

— — —. 2009. "Main Direction for Improvement in the Unified State Examination Tests in 2008–2009". Moscow. http://www.fipi.ru/binaries/342/napravleniya%20sov.doc.

Froumin, I., Pinskaya, M., Kosaretsky, S., Plahotnuk, T. 2011. "Schools in Difficult Social Environments: 'Drowning' and 'Struggling'." Presentation handouts. Institute for Educational Research, National Research University—Higher School of Economics. Moscow.

Organization for Economic Co-operation and Development (OECD). 2010. Education at a Glance 2010: OECD Indicators. http://www.oecd.org/edu/eag2010

— — —. 2010. *PISA-2009 Key Findings*. Paris: OECD.

Simakova, S. 2009 "Invisible Children." Children's Rights Commissionerfor the President of the Russian Federation. http://www.google.com/url?sa=t&rct=j&q=&esrc=s&source=web&cd=4&ved=0CDQQFjAD&url=http%3A%2F%2Fwww.rfdeti.ru%2Ffiles%2F1270213267_novisible_child.doc&ei=OJPDTojXHYPv0gHLqNX-oDg&usg=AFQjCNFGsZ8B4sZ0fIyjtnynAwNCHNZS2g&sig2=08o3KKRvBd8-F25MGOSlLA

Soldatova, V., Kuvshinova, A. 2006. "Assessment of Actual and Potential Consequences of Reforms Implemented within Project of Education System Reform for Teachers." Federal Service for State Statistics of Russia, Moscow.

World Bank. 2010. "Social Expenditure Review." World Bank, Washington, DC.

CHAPTER 4

Vocational Education and Training

Current Situation and Trends

Coverage

Vocational education and training (VET) plays an important role in providing the skills, knowledge, and competences needed in the labor market. In 2000–10 the number of students studying in educational institutions providing initial vocational education and training (IVET) decreased by 41.4 percent, lowering the coverage ratio to 21.5 percent (down from 22.3 percent in 2000). However, due to negative demographic tendencies coverage ratio to IVET has been increasing beginning from 2008 (figure 4.1).

The number of students studying in secondary vocational education and training (SVET) institutions dropped less significantly during that period—only by 10 percent. The situation with coverage ratios parallels the demographic trends in Russia (figure 4.2). These demographic changes will have a further impact on the vocational education and training system in Russia.

Institutional Structure and Scale

Facing the problem of the decline in the corresponding age population, state authorities intended to restructure the present network of state VET institutions. The number of IVET institutions has changed dramatically decreasing by almost 40 percent in 2000–10

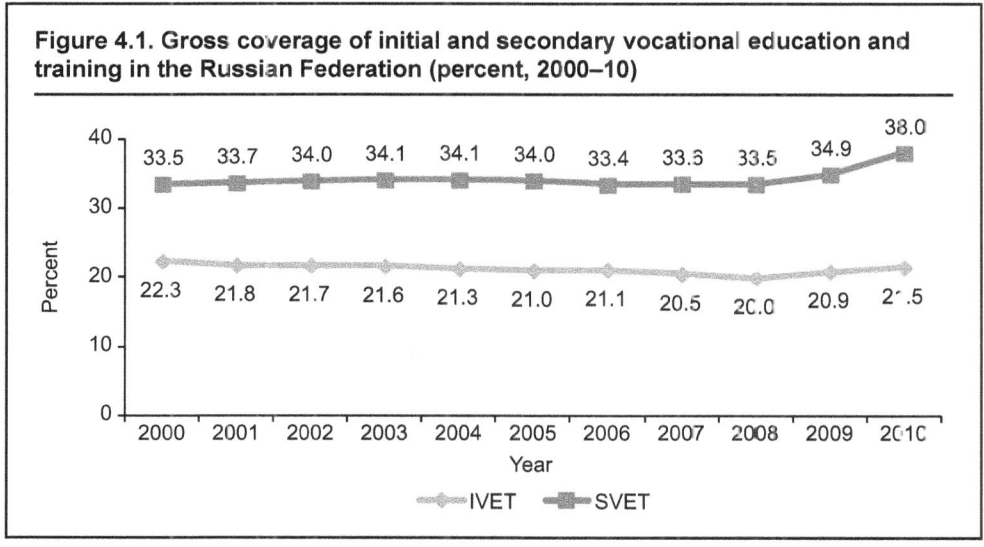

Figure 4.1. Gross coverage of initial and secondary vocational education and training in the Russian Federation (percent, 2000–10)

Source: Authors' calculations based on data of the Federal Service for State Statistics of the Russian Federation.
Note: Figure shows ratio of students studying in IVET institution to age cohort 15–17 years and ratio of students studying in SVET institution to age cohort 17–19 years.

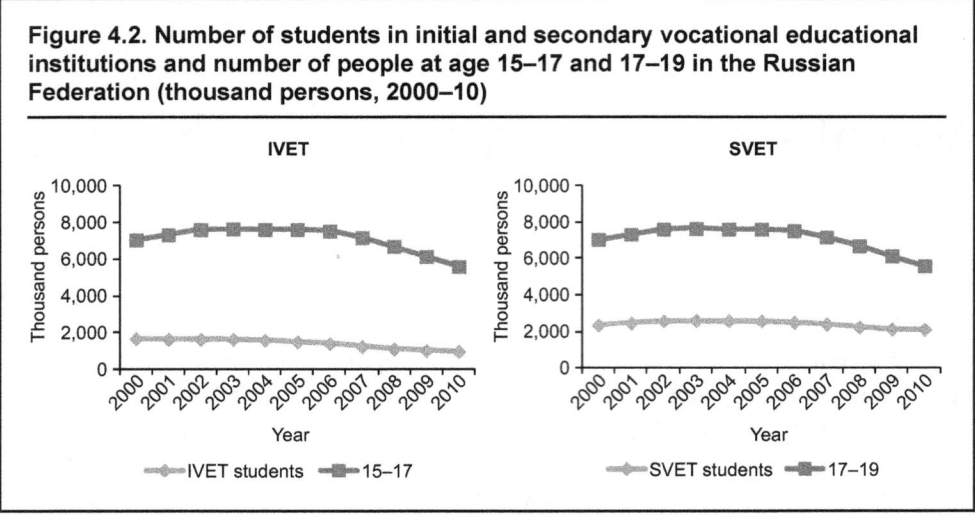

Figure 4.2. Number of students in initial and secondary vocational educational institutions and number of people at age 15–17 and 17–19 in the Russian Federation (thousand persons, 2000–10)

Source: Authors' calculations based on data of the Federal Service for State Statistics of the Russian Federation.

(figure 4.3). In 2010 by law the merging process of initial and secondary vocational institution networks started, and in 2010 the IVET system was abolished.

Cadres

The number of teaching staff in SVET institutions has increased in line with the growth of the network of SVET institutions (their number increased by 15 percent in 2000–10). Teaching staff in IVET institutions were to be terminated as a consequence of the closure of educational institutions (figures 4.4 and 4.5). Currently the staff not classified

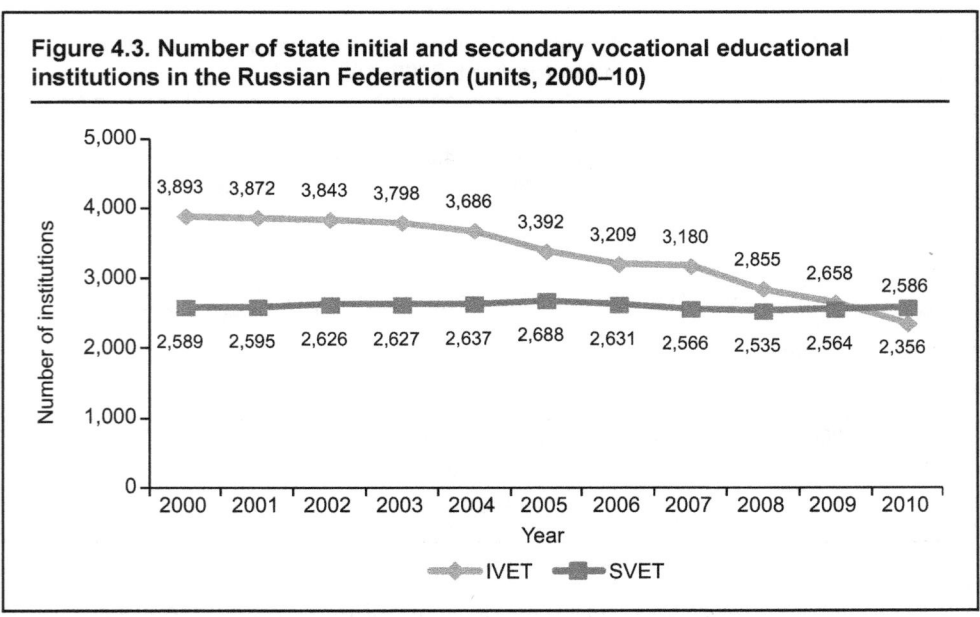

Figure 4.3. Number of state initial and secondary vocational educational institutions in the Russian Federation (units, 2000–10)

Source: Federal Service for State Statistics of the Russian Federation.

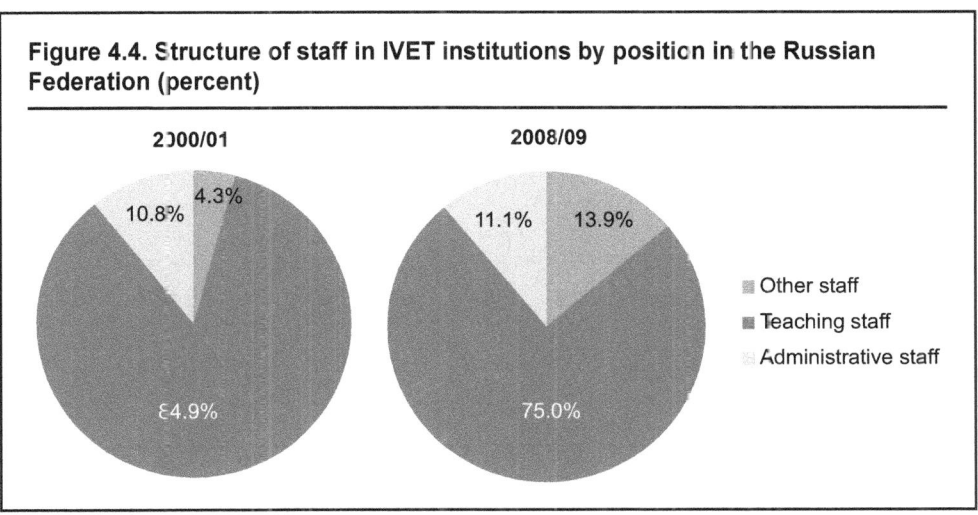

Figure 4.4. Structure of staff in IVET institutions by position in the Russian Federation (percent)

2000/01: 4.3%, 10.8%, 84.9%
2008/09: 13.9%, 11.1%, 75.0%

Legend: Other staff; Teaching staff; Administrative staff

Source: Authors' calculations based on data of the Federal Service for State Statistics of the Russian Federation.

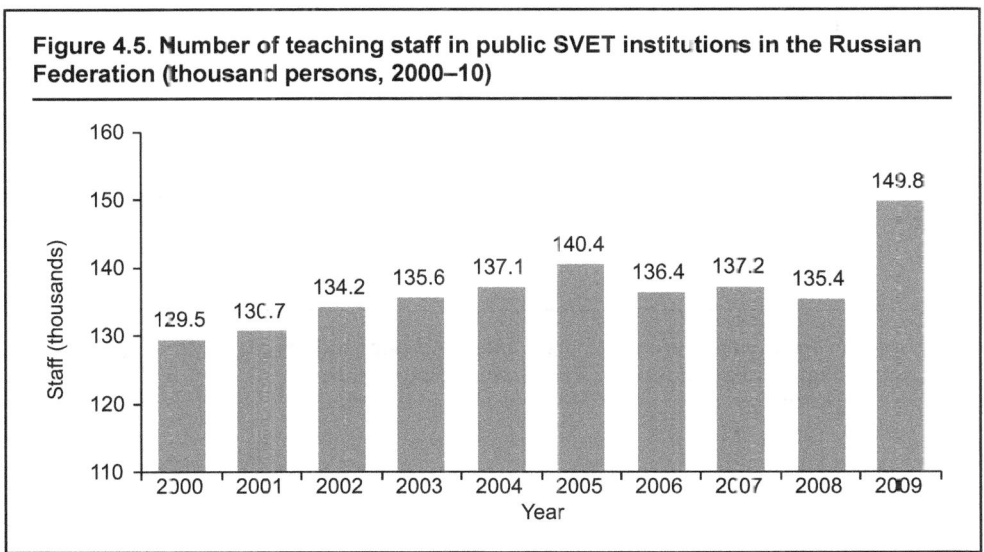

Figure 4.5. Number of teaching staff in public SVET institutions in the Russian Federation (thousand persons, 2000–10)

Year	2000	2001	2002	2003	2004	2005	2006	2007	2008	2009
Staff (thousands)	129.5	130.7	134.2	135.6	137.1	140.4	136.4	137.2	135.4	149.8

Source: Federal Service for State Statistics of the Russian Federation.

as instructional personnel (staff other than teaching staff, teachers' aides and research assistants) represent on average slightly less than a quarter of the total teaching and nonteaching staff in initial vocational institutions.

Despite institutional changes in the VET system, the student-teacher ratio in both sectors has not changed significantly. Internationally, Russia is close to the European estimates of student-teaching staff ratio in vocational education: in postsecondary nontertiary education (equivalent to Russian IVET) OECD average is 13.8 and the EU19 average 13.2; in tertiary education type-B (equivalent to Russian SVET) the OECD average is 19.7 and the EU19 average 12.8 (2008 data) (OECD 2010) (figure 4.6).

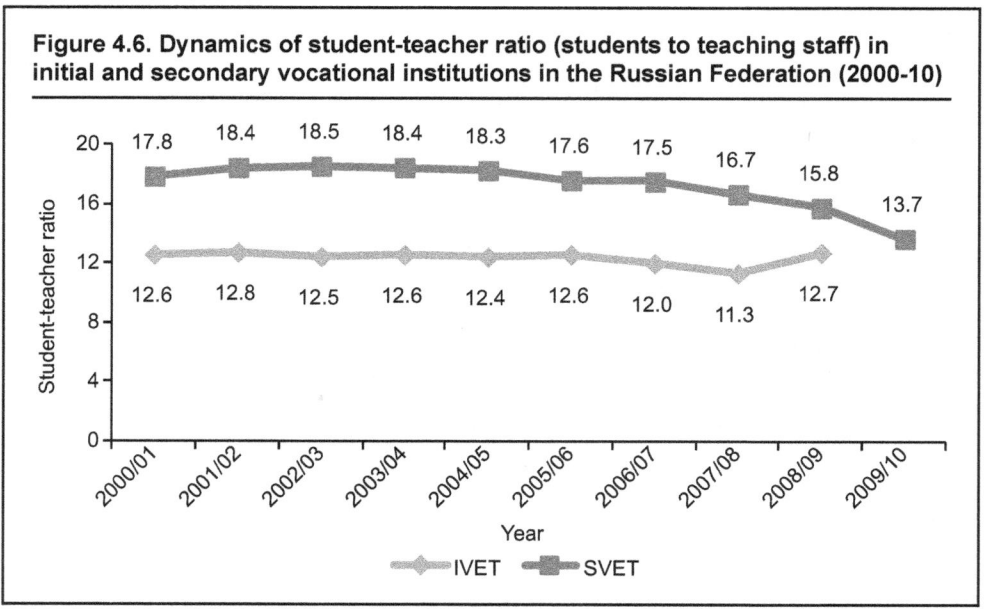

Figure 4.6. Dynamics of student-teacher ratio (students to teaching staff) in initial and secondary vocational institutions in the Russian Federation (2000-10)

Source: Authors' calculations based on data of the Federal Service for State Statistics of the Russian Federation.
Note: Information regarding the number of personnel in IVET in 2010 is not available.

Financing

The volume of government spending on vocational education has significantly increased over the past seven years, growing three-fold from RUR 54.5 billion (US$1.8 billion) in 2003 to RUR 169 billion (US$5.6 billion) in 2009 (figure 4.7). This translates into an aver-

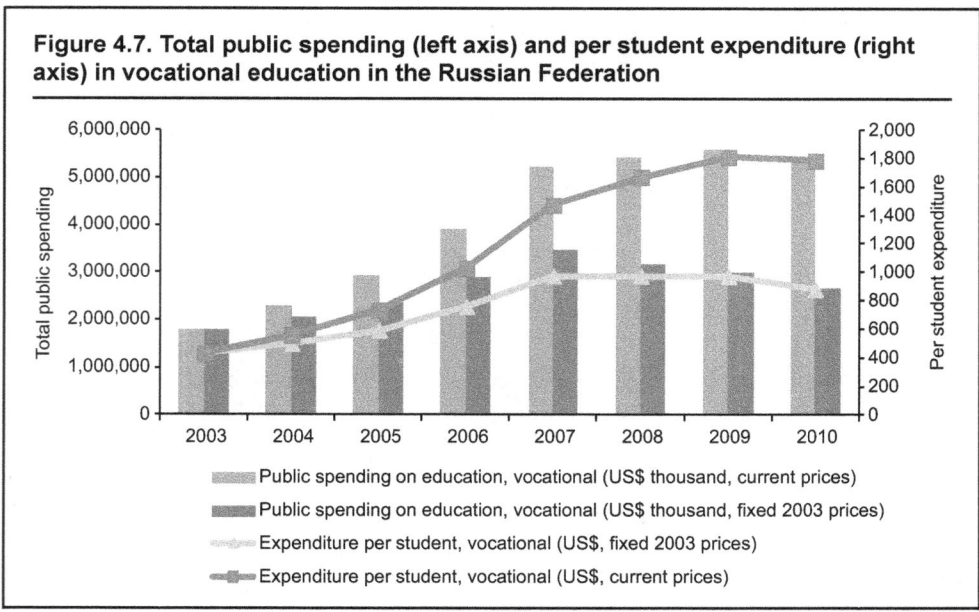

Figure 4.7. Total public spending (left axis) and per student expenditure (right axis) in vocational education in the Russian Federation

Source: Authors' calculations based on data of the Federal Service for State Statistics, Treasury, and the Central Bank of the Russian Federation.

age annual increase of 21.0 percent (14.2 percent for IVET, 27.6 percent for SVET). In 2010 VET financing decreased by 3 percent down to 163.7 (US$5.4 billion). In fixed 2003 prices the decrease in financing between 2009 and 2010 was even more significant—11.7 percent. This trend is most likely connected with changes occurring in the vocational education system, including the decline in the number of students and closure of vocational schools.

The proportion of GDP per capita earmarked for vocational education increased from 14.4 percent in 2003 to almost 20 percent in 2009 and dropped to 17.3 percent in 2010 (top line in figure 4.8). The share of public expenditure on vocational education in total public expenditure on education between 2003 and 2010 has been decreasing (bottom line in figure 4.8).

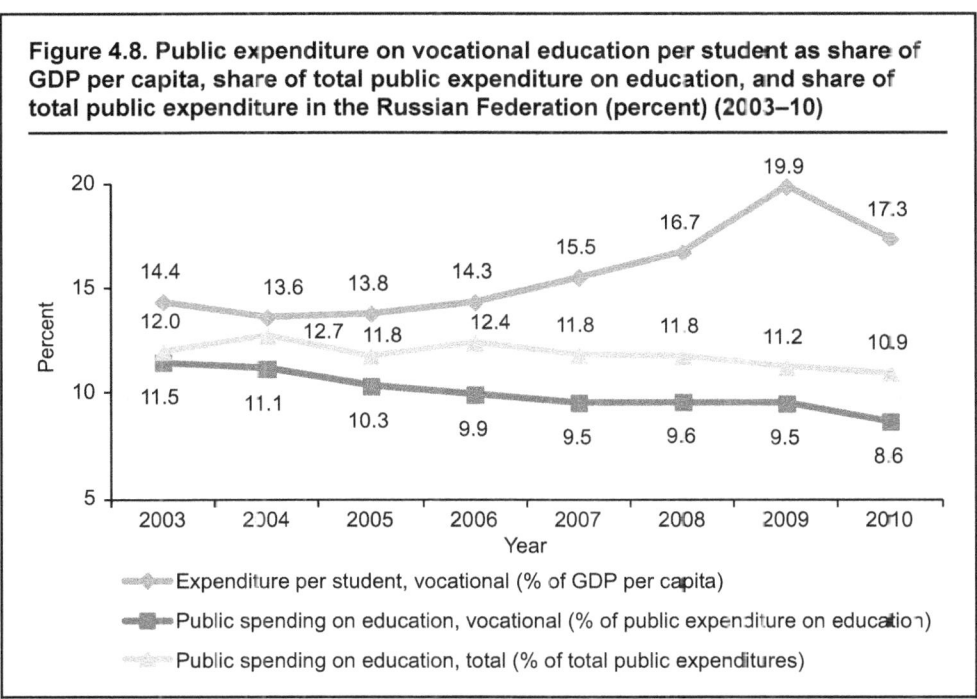

Figure 4.8. Public expenditure on vocational education per student as share of GDP per capita, share of total public expenditure on education, and share of total public expenditure in the Russian Federation (percent) (2003–10)

Source: Authors' calculations based on data of the Federal Service for State Statistics, and Treasury of the Russian Federation.

Regional Differentiation

Data on educational expenditures on vocational programs show wide variations between Russian regions in their levels of total public expenditure on initial and secondary VET programs as a percentage of GRP. Spending ranges from 0.03 percent to 1.27 percent for IVET and from 0.02 percent to 0.68 percent for SVET (figure 4.9).

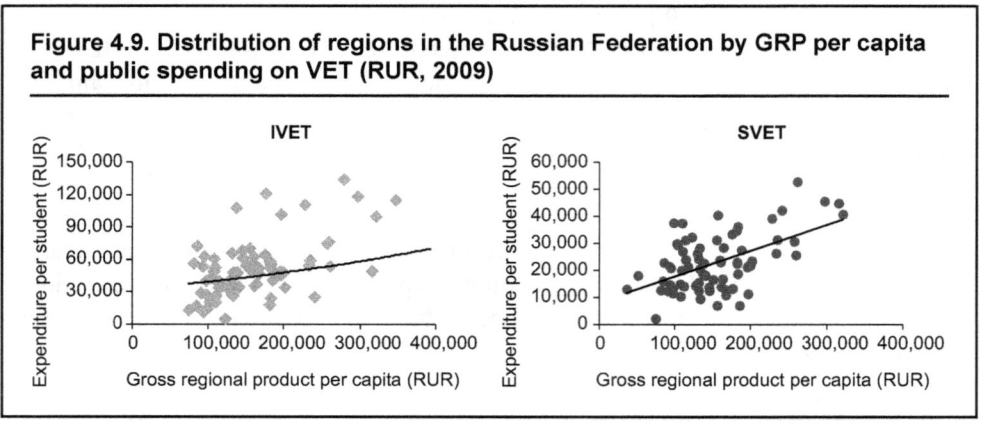

Figure 4.9. Distribution of regions in the Russian Federation by GRP per capita and public spending on VET (RUR, 2009)

Source: Authors' calculations based on data of the Federal Service for State Statistics, Treasury, and the Central Bank of the Russian Federation.

Recent and Ongoing Reforms

Decentralization of Governance and Finance

Intensive regionalization of vocational schools and colleges began in 2005 in order to adjust the structure of education and training in educational institutions to the needs of regional economies (figure 4.10). Nevertheless, there is still a large number of institutions under federal subordination (1,039 out of 2,535 public SVET institutions[2]). Not all regions can carry the burden of providing financial support to newly transferred vocational institutions as the federal government does not in all cases provide subventions to those regions. However, according to a federal government initiative all institutions are to be transferred in 2012.

Introduction of Qualification Framework

The National Qualification Framework was created as a result of teamwork of the Federal Institute for Education Development and National Agency for Qualifications Development. It is a very important document, but it has a recommendatory character. The Ministry of Education and Science of the Russian Federation did not confirm the standards of vocational and higher education connected with learning outcomes. The Russian Union of Industrialists and Entrepreneurs coordinates the work on the creation of professional standards by employers and faces difficulties in conveying the importance of this work to employers.

The work on creation of the regional centers of professional certification has not start-

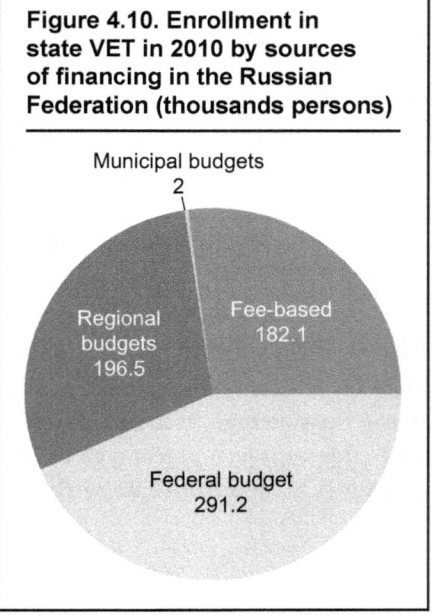

Figure 4.10. Enrollment in state VET in 2010 by sources of financing in the Russian Federation (thousands persons)

Source: Federal Service for State Statistics of the Russian Federation.

ed. The idea is to create an external independent quality assurance of vocational and higher education. This is possible only on the basis of graduates' certification results with the participation of regional employers. One more problem is that current documents do not consider the European Credit Transfer and Accumulation System (ECTS). Creation of educational standards precedes creation of professional standards. All this means that results should be corrected, but there are no regulatory procedures for standards correction.

Introduction of Applied Bachelor Programs

For this project the European idea (as in Finland and Germany) was used of creating applied bachelor programs for vocational education institutions such as colleges and technical schools. The Ministry of Education and Science of the Russian Federation announced in the middle of 2009 a competition for development and implementation of such programs.

But according to the Russian legislative base, only higher education institutions may implement such programs. Colleges have no rights to provide bachelor-level programs, so this incentive may cause a fast outflow of students from independent colleges to colleges under university control or to universities themselves.

Government Programs to Support Development of Regional VET Systems

The government intends to improve the professional and vocational education system through support of regional programs for VET system development on a competitive basis. As said above the process of transferring federal vocational institutions to regional subordination is almost completed in many regions of Russia. Currently the government is supporting regional programs of VET system development that best adjust education systems to the needs of regional economies. The support includes co-financing from the Federal Ministry of Education and Science and provision of assistance in dissemination of regional experience on a national level.

Key Problems and Challenges

Access and Quality

The Russian system of vocational education is plagued by two major problems: (i) the large number of relatively small vocational schools and (ii) narrow specialist offerings. The Soviet system trained students in narrowly specialized programs for jobs in a planned economy. The economy has changed dramatically, but the training system has not kept pace. At present, the system of vocational education is not relevant to the labor market's needs and thus supplies a labor force that does not measure up to business-sector demand. Top managers of enterprises often complain that they have to provide in-plant retraining to every newly employed young specialist. The fact that the regional labor market has become inundated with graduates in economic and legal disciplines and their supply by far exceeds the demand from employers is substantial evidence of the labor market distortions. This, in its turn, has led to an undersupply of those graduates who skills are really necessary in the labor market: 5.5 percent of graduates from vocational institutions in Russia registered in placement services as unemployed in 2010.[3] In reality the situation could be more tragic as very small share of young people apply to placement services in case they do not get a job after their graduation.[4]

There appears to be a serious gap/mismatch between the skills demanded by employers and the skills provided by the education and training system. The reason for the existing gap/mismatch appears to lie on the quality side of education and training, that is, inadequate quality of education of graduates from educational institutions. This is further exemplified by the fact that labor market expansion capacity appears to have been exhausted and this combined with the changes to the demographics (the aging population) is indicating a serious and tightening bottleneck for the growth.

The key to prosperity in a modern economy with intense local and global competition experiencing rapid technological change is a properly educated and skilled workforce producing high value-added, knowledge-intensive goods and services.

Regional TVET systems are in urgent need of reform. Such need comes from a range of problems faced by education systems and institutions. First is continuous underfinancing of VET institutions over a period of almost two previous decades (Spiridonova 2011). This caused significant developmental retardation of VET systems in comparison to modern requirements of regional labor markets, obsolescence of general funds, and decreasing attractiveness of VET among young people. Second is the continuous mismatch between the number of students studying in educational institutions, their specializations, and real needs of the regional economy. This mismatch has caused regions to suffer significant economic losses and social expenses (Kochetkov 2011). Currently many regions are trying to adjust the VET system to the labor market needs. However, they lack a vision for a strategic program and the developmental capacity to do it.

There is a continuing need to develop a strategy for in-depth reform of the entire vocational education and training system, including how its various components interact with one other and how they link to general and higher education.

Policy Options

The system of vocational education is not relevant to the labor market needs and thus trains a labor force that does not meet the demands of the business sector. The contradictions of the present VET system could cause it to lose its position in the market of educational services and be replaced with corporate retraining centers. At the same time, demand for VET-trained workers capable of working in modern industry using new complicated technical equipment is increasing in the regional economies.

The vocational education system has to be capable of providing two types of services to support competitiveness of a country or region. First, it should be able to equip students with key general and technical skills and knowledge. Second, it should provide opportunities for constant renewing, updating, and adjustment of the skills.

Government policy measures should taken both on federal and regional levels:

- On the federal level the Russian government should continue to support (mostly financially) effective reforms being implemented in the regions—reform "from the bottom."
- On the regional level the following should be done:
  - Conduct monitoring and evaluation activities for defining most crucial problems of VET systems.

- Optimize the network of vocational education institutions for modern economy. For example, adjust the VET network as well as training and education provided in VET institutions to the needs of local economies.
- Modernize organizational and economical managing mechanisms in regional VET systems on the basis of budgeting focused on result principles—"financing for results."
- Create organizational and economical mechanisms for permanent updating of the curricula and educational technologies.
- Implement a public-private partnership strategy of quality management in vocational education on the basis of activity results monitoring and using an external quality assurance system.

Notes

1. Estimation based on data of Treasury of the Russian Federation.
2. According to data of Federal Service of State Statistics.
3. According to data of Ministry of Education and Science of the Russian Federation.
4. According to data of Ministry of Labor of the Russian Federation.

References

Federal Service for State Statistics of Russia. 2010. *Statistical Yearbook of the Russian Federation—2010*. Moscow.

Kochetkov, A. 2011. "Professional Education and Labor Market: Problems of Interaction." Institute of Sociology, Russian Academy of Sciences. http://www.isras.ru/files/File/Socis/2011-5/Kochetov.pdf, pp. 82–90.

Spiridonova, G. 2011. "Problems of Adaptation of VET Graduates to the Labor Market." State Budgetary Institution of Further Professional Education of the Republic of Adygea. http://www.aripk.ru/pedsovet2008/section/konsult/newdocs/nach_i_sr_pr_obr/adapt.doc.

CHAPTER 5

Higher Education

Current Situation and Trends

Coverage

The number of students pursuing higher education in Russia has significantly increased over the past 18 years, growing 2.5 times from 2.8 million in 1990 to 7.1 million in 2010 (figure 5.1). This translates into an average annual increase of about 5 percent. Gross coverage by higher education doubled over this period. However, a closer look at the data reveals that the expansion has been significantly due to the growth of the number of students studying in private institutions—a unique feature of the post-Soviet era (figure 5.2).

An interesting feature of the Russian higher education system is that starting from 2000 the number of entrants to educational institutions has exceeded the number of school leavers (figure 5.3). This reflects that not only graduates from schools are applying to higher education institution but also leavers from vocational schools in order to increase their educational level.

Looking at the number of entrants to higher education institutions it should be noted that beginning from the same year (2000) the number of students applying to fee-

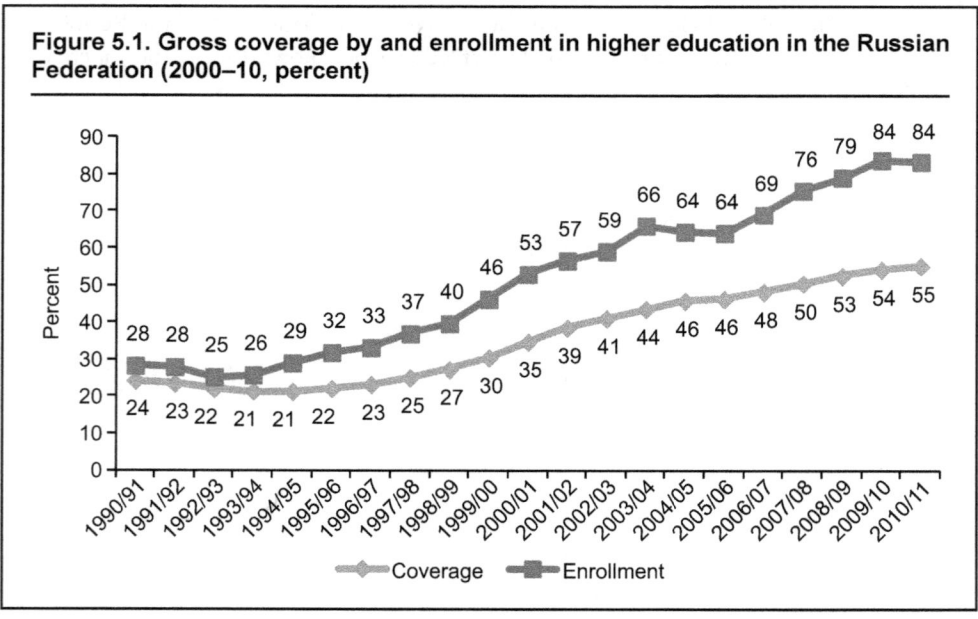

Figure 5.1. Gross coverage by and enrollment in higher education in the Russian Federation (2000–10, percent)

Source: Authors' calculations based on data of the Federal Service for State Statistics of the Russian Federation.
Note: Figure shows ratio of students studying in higher education institutions to 17-to-22-year-olds; and ratio of entrants to higher education institutions to 17-year-olds.

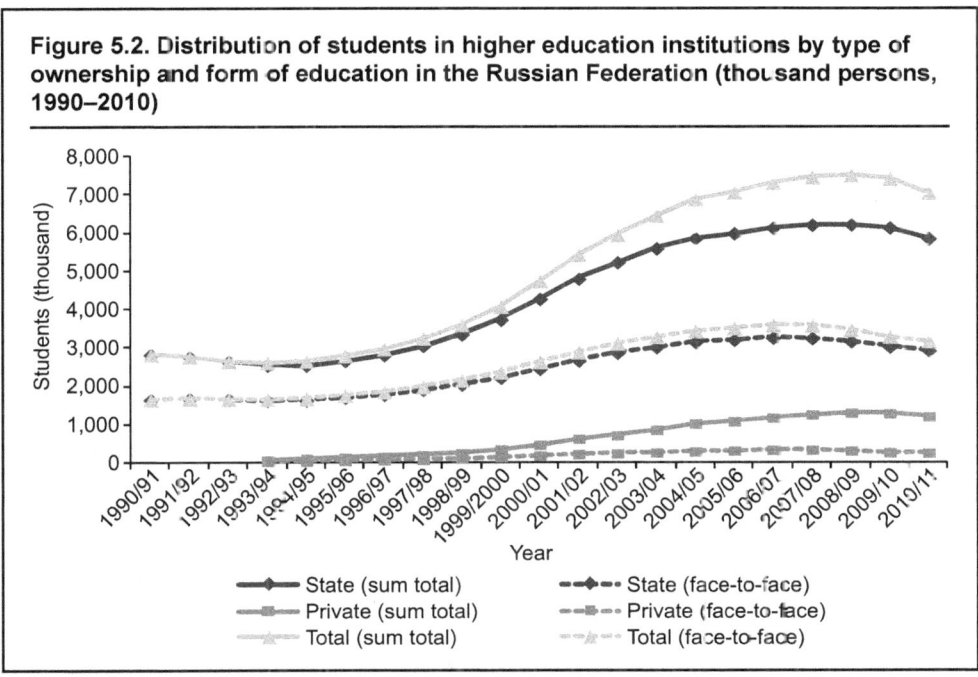

Figure 5.2. Distribution of students in higher education institutions by type of ownership and form of education in the Russian Federation (thousand persons, 1990–2010)

Source: Authors' calculations based on data of the Federal Service for State Statistics of the Russian Federation.

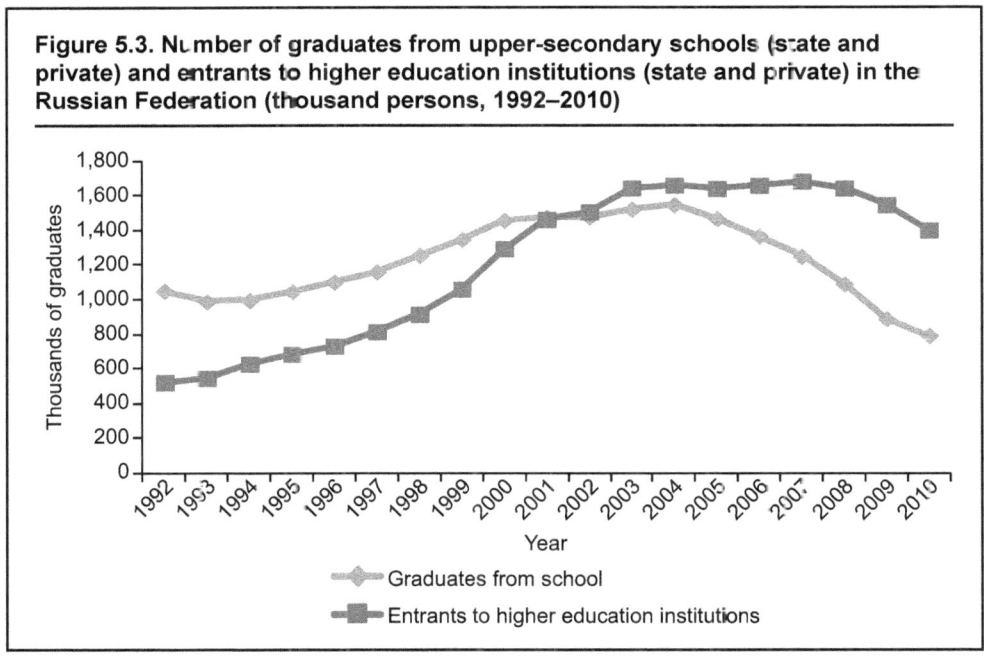

Figure 5.3. Number of graduates from upper-secondary schools (state and private) and entrants to higher education institutions (state and private) in the Russian Federation (thousand persons, 1992–2010)

Source: Federal Service for State Statistics of the Russian Federation.

based services at educational institutions has been exceeding the number of students applying to state-funded places (figure 5.4). This is quite alarming as fee-based training in universities has been mostly in areas that are popular among students (economics,

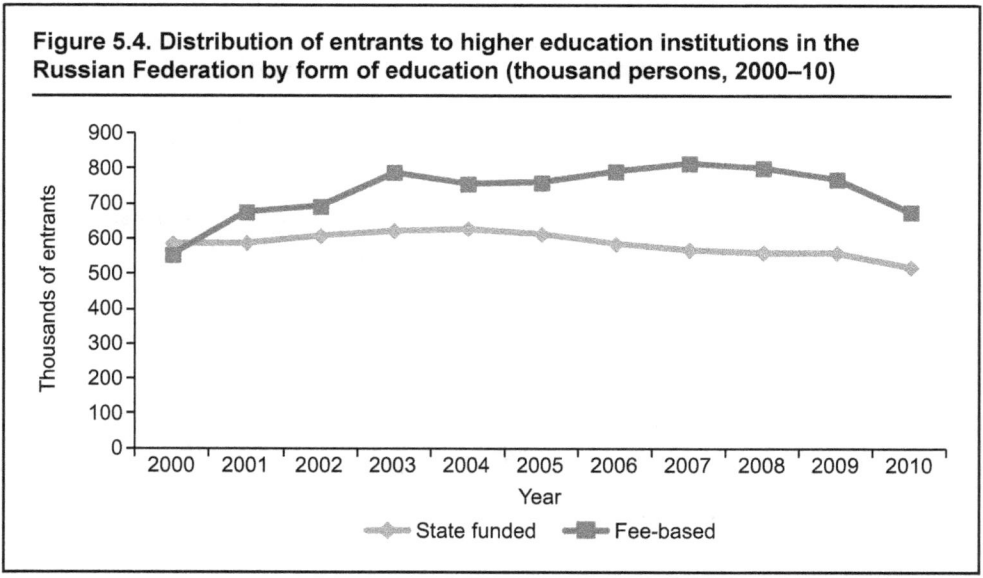

Figure 5.4. Distribution of entrants to higher education institutions in the Russian Federation by form of education (thousand persons, 2000–10)

Source: Federal Service for State Statistics of the Russian Federation.

management, law) but that already in low demand by employers due to overproduction of such specialists in previous years.

Institutional Structure and Scale

The network of higher education institutions has experienced significant growth, increasing by more than 15 percent in 2000–10. However, a closer look at the data reveals that much of the expansion comes from the growing number of nonstate higher education institutions. Their number increased by 29 percent (against 8 percent growth in the number of state HEIs) (figure 5.5).

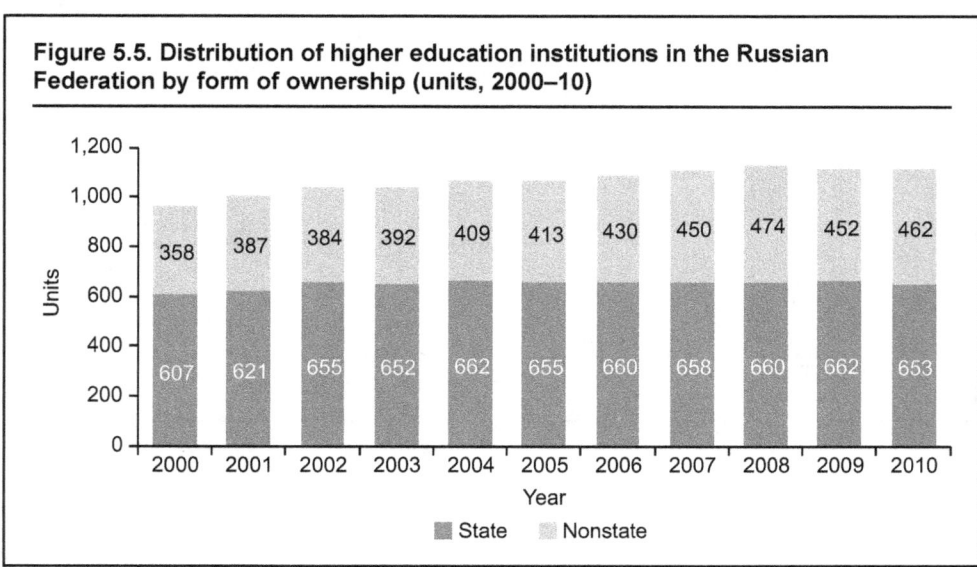

Figure 5.5. Distribution of higher education institutions in the Russian Federation by form of ownership (units, 2000–10)

Source: Federal Service for State Statistics of the Russian Federation.

Higher education has a hierarchical management system that includes three levels: federal, regional, and municipal. Distribution of higher education institutions by level of subordination is shown in figure 5.6 and by type in figure 5.7.

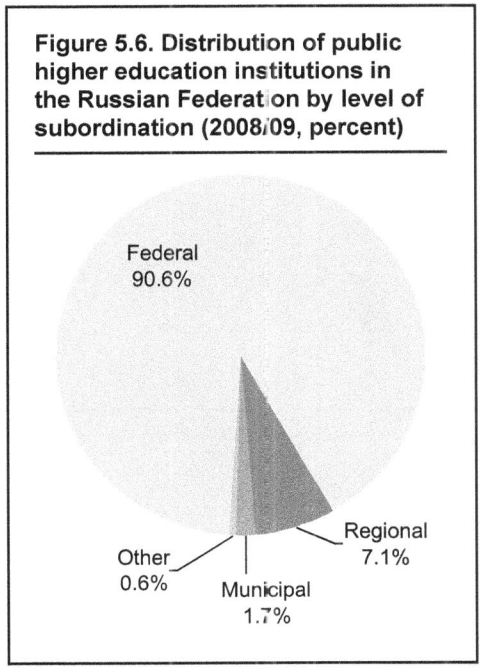

Figure 5.6. Distribution of public higher education institutions in the Russian Federation by level of subordination (2008/09, percent)

Source: Authors' calculations based on data of the Federal Service for State Statistics of the Russian Federation.

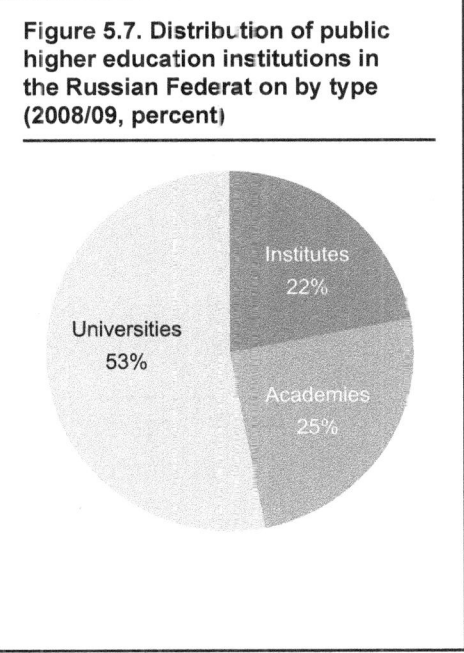

Figure 5.7. Distribution of public higher education institutions in the Russian Federation by type (2008/09, percent)

Source: Authors' calculations based on data of the Federal Service for State Statistics of the Russian Federation.

The network of higher education institutions is supplemented by a widely spread network of institution branches in the regions of Russia. In the 2008/09 academic year there were 1,663 branches of higher education institutions including 1,102 branches of public HEIs, and 561 of private. Thus, each higher education institution has on average 1.5 branches (1.7 in the public sector of the higher education system, and 1.2 in the private sector).

Cadres

In higher education, staff not classified as instructional personnel represent on average nearly 20 percent of the total teaching and nonteaching staff (40 percent for tertiary education in OECD), which may indicate of high potential for science instruction of Russian higher education institutions (figure 5.8).

Financing

This section presents data on expenditure per student in higher education as well as total government expenditure on higher education as a percentage of GDP—the two key indicators for the financing of higher education. Unfortunately, a lack of data limits the information on private funding even though it is also an important factor in financing higher education.

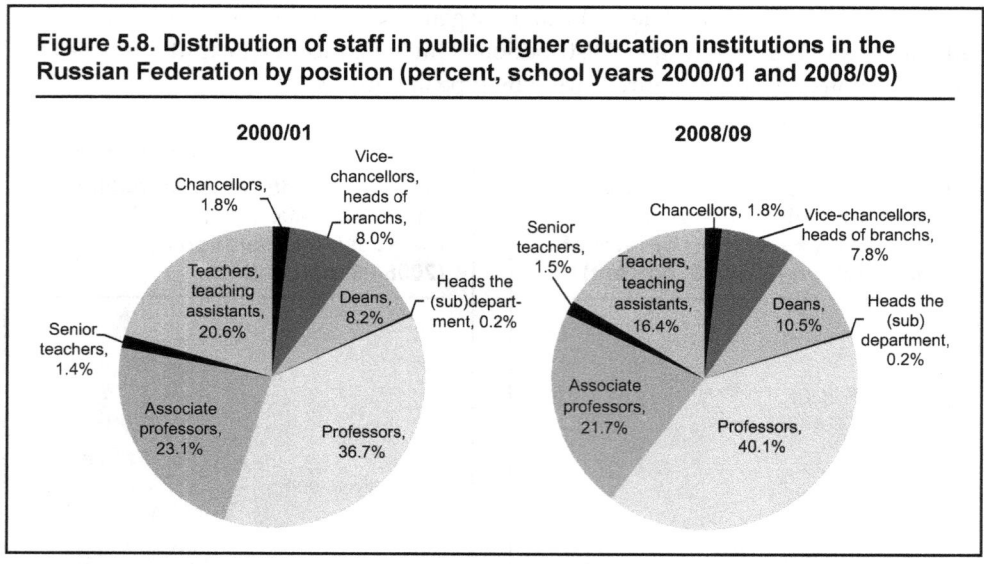

Figure 5.8. Distribution of staff in public higher education institutions in the Russian Federation by position (percent, school years 2000/01 and 2008/09)

Source: Authors' calculations based on data of the Federal Service for State Statistics of the Russian Federation.

The volume of government spending on higher education has significantly increased over the past five years, growing almost six-fold from RUR 61.2 billion (US$2.0 billion) in 2003 to RUR 377.8 billion (US$12.3 billion) in 2010. This translates into an average annual increase of 30.7 percent. However, in fixed 2003 prices the increase of higher education financing has been much less: the spending increased three times, which can still be considered as a significant change (see figures 5.9 and 5.10).

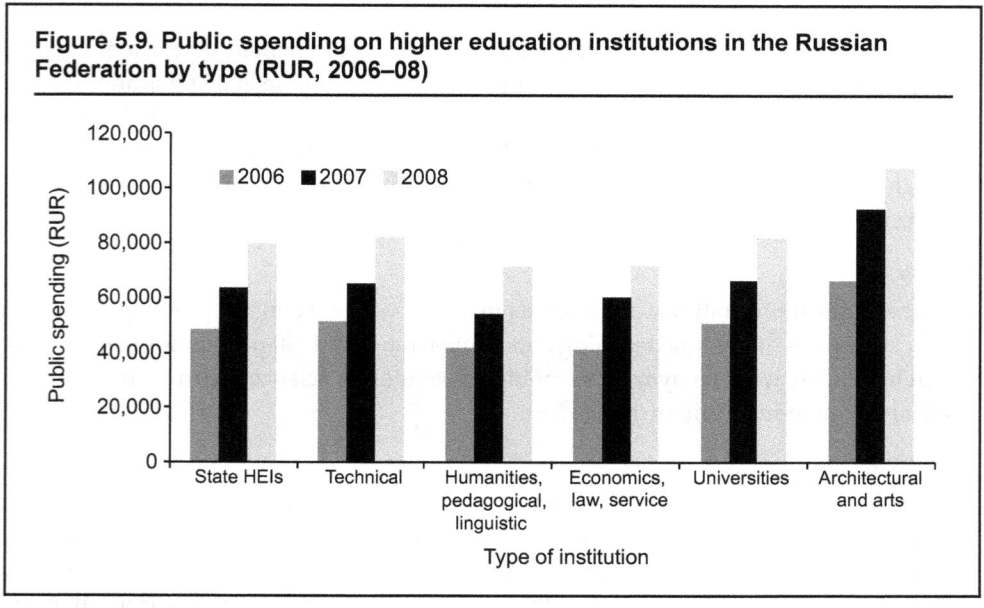

Figure 5.9. Public spending on higher education institutions in the Russian Federation by type (RUR, 2006–08)

Source: Authors' calculations based on the data of Abankina, 2009.

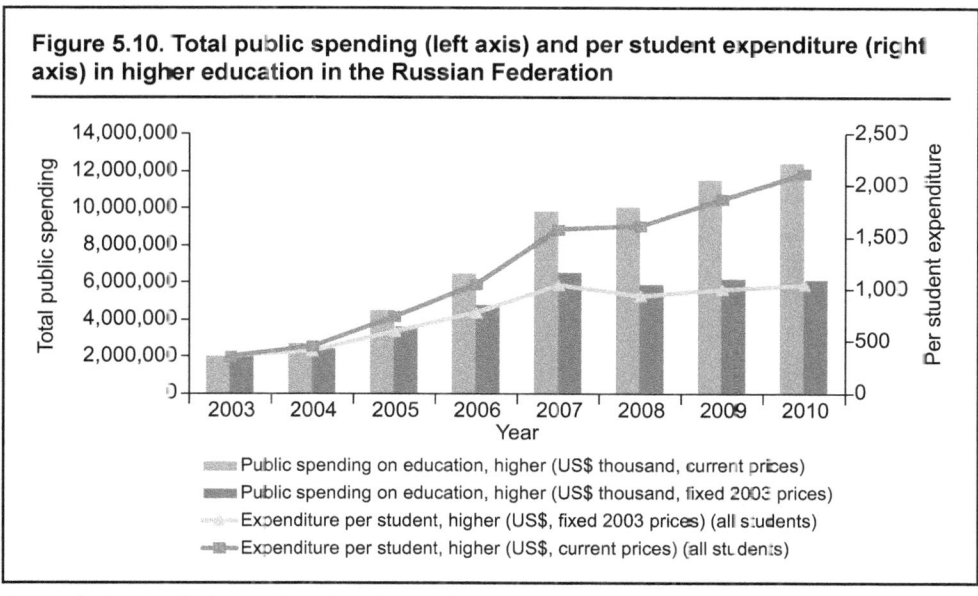

Figure 5.10. Total public spending (left axis) and per student expenditure (right axis) in higher education in the Russian Federation

Source: Authors' calculations based on data of the Federal Service for State Statistics, the Central Bank, and Treasury of the Russian Federation.

Public spending on education is relatively stable as a share of total public spending. Per student investment on state higher education institutions (as a share of GDP per capita) increased from 12.0 percent in 2003 to 20.6 percent in 2010 (figure 5.11). Moreover, as can be seen from the data, higher education became a higher priority in the area of education financing. The share of spending on higher education in total public spending on education increased from 12.9 percent to 19.9 percent during that period.

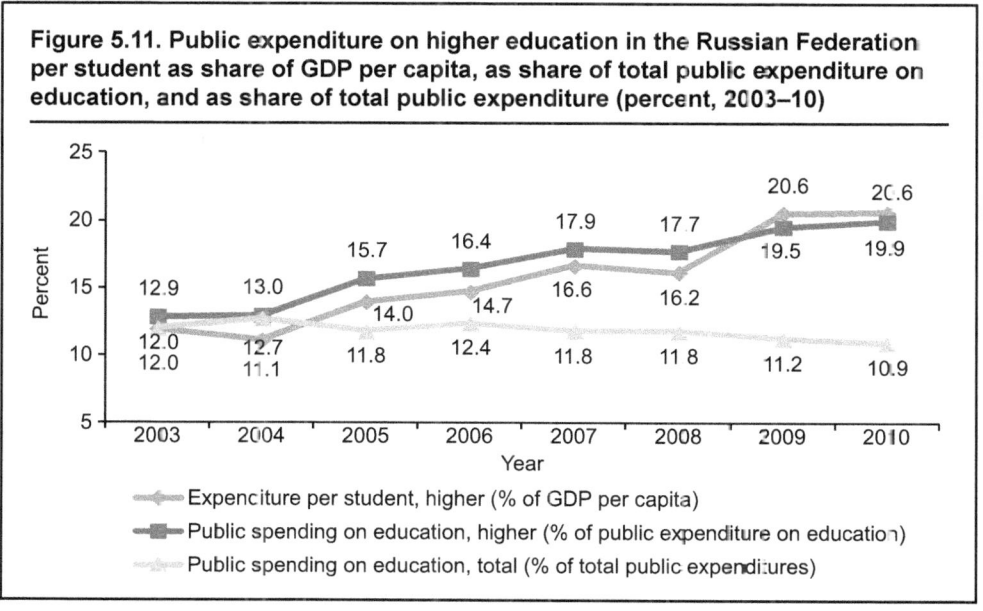

Figure 5.11. Public expenditure on higher education in the Russian Federation per student as share of GDP per capita, as share of total public expenditure on education, and as share of total public expenditure (percent, 2003–10)

Source: Authors' calculations based on data of Federal Service for State Statistics, and Treasury of the Russian Federation.

Looking outside Russia, OECD countries as a whole spend US$12,907 annually per tertiary student (OECD 2010). On average, OECD countries spend nearly twice as much per student at the tertiary level as at the primary level. Russia also spends, on average, two times more on educational institutions per student at the tertiary level than at the primary level (figure 5.12).

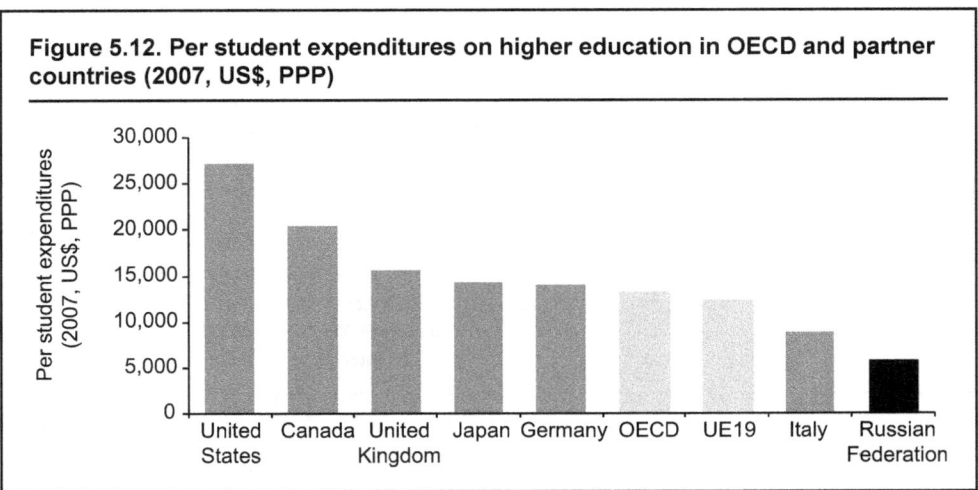

Figure 5.12. Per student expenditures on higher education in OECD and partner countries (2007, US$, PPP)

Source: Authors' calculations based on OECD 2010.

Regional Differentiation

State HEIs are mostly financed from the federal budget with only 3.5 percent of total funding in 2010 coming from regional budgets. There is great regional variation in staff salaries. The lowest salaries are found in the Southwest regions, ranging from about RUR 9,037 in Karachay-Cherkessia Republic to RUR 12,070 in Kalmyk Republic in 2010 (the Russian average is RUR 21,319) (figure 5.13). Notably high salaries are found in the

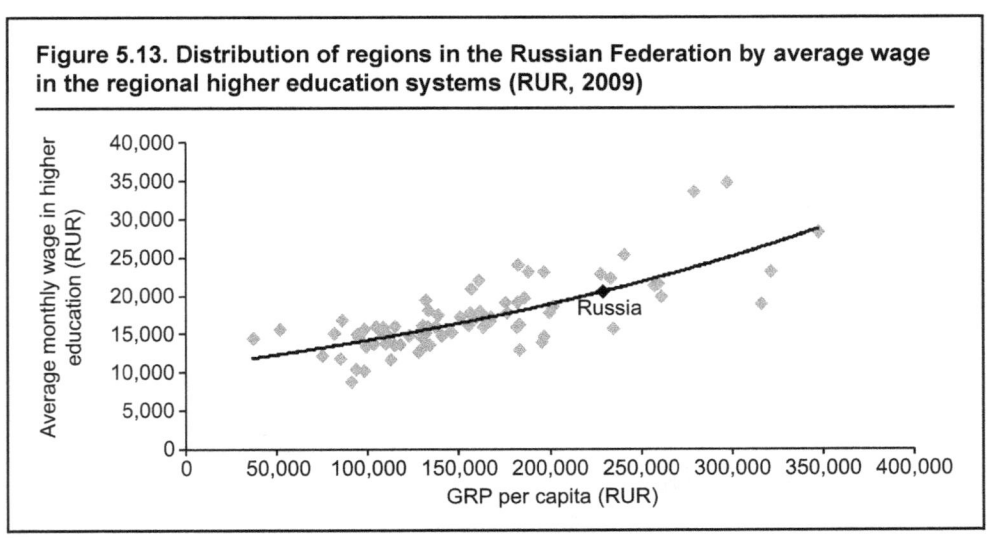

Figure 5.13. Distribution of regions in the Russian Federation by average wage in the regional higher education systems (RUR, 2009)

Source: Authors' calculations based on data of the Federal Service for State Statistics of the Russian Federation.

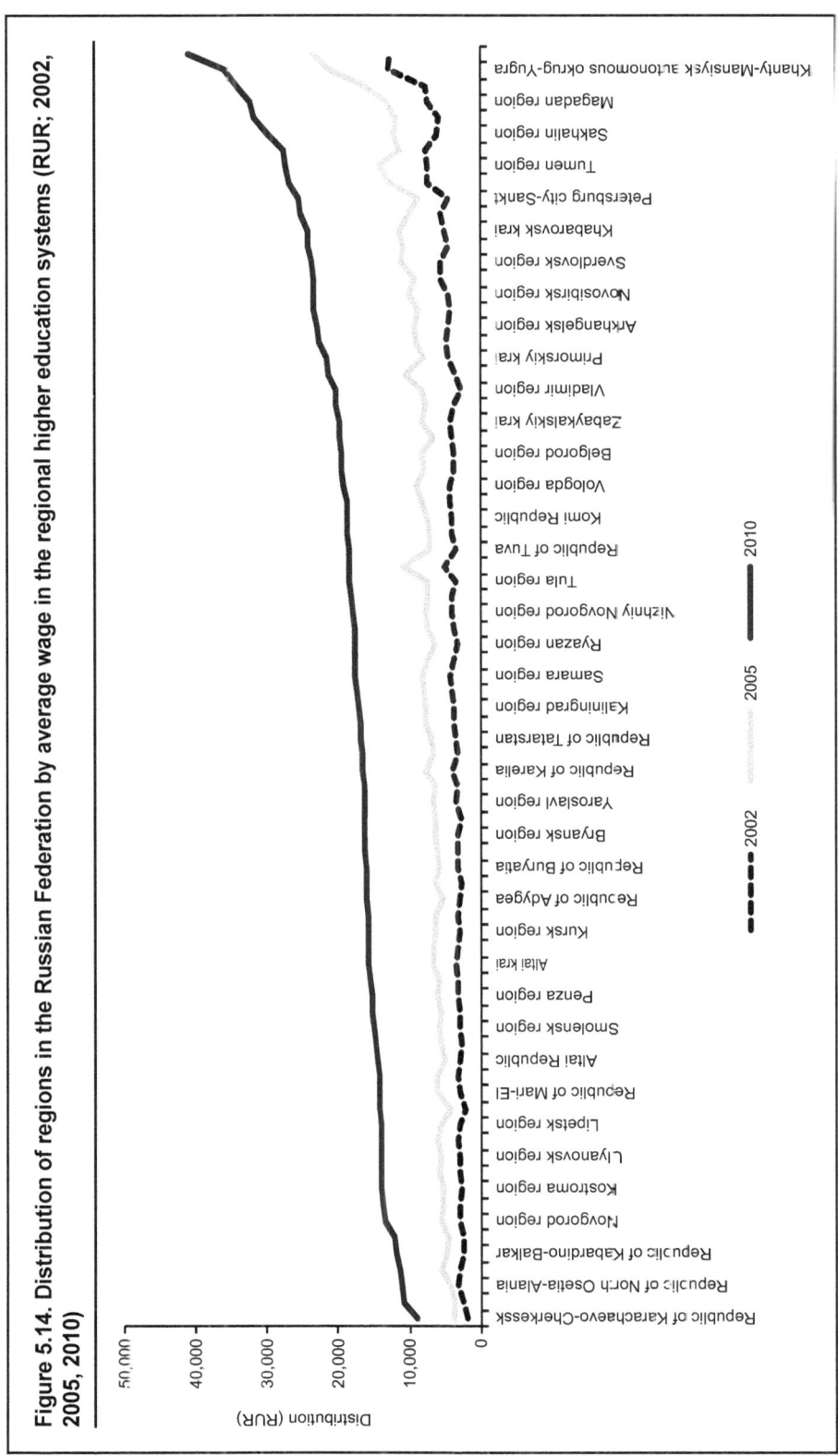

Figure 5.14. Distribution of regions in the Russian Federation by average wage in the regional higher education systems (RUR; 2002, 2005, 2010)

Source: Federal Service for State Statistics of the Russian Federation.

Northern regions with oil-dependent economies: Yamalo-Nenets AO (RUR 40,949) and Khanty-Mansiysk AO (RUR 35,924). These regional variations may be considered good since they are responses to local labor markets.

Higher education salaries in the regions of Russia have significantly increased over the past nine years, growing almost four-fold from RUR 4,310 in 2002 to RUR 21,319 in 2010. This translates into an average annual increase of 22.3 percent in real terms (see figure 5.14 on previous page).

Recent and Ongoing Reforms

New Educational Standards

It was decided that, starting in September 2010, new educational standards in higher education would be implemented. As in other levels of education, standards are oriented on learning outcomes written in terms of competences. Universities can independently select half of their courses and curricula, and must offer optional courses in every educational program. Course offerings also are oriented on the independent study of students: up to 50 percent of learning time is reserved for student self-learning.

Federal and National Research Universities

The main goals of forming *federal universities* is the development of the higher education system on the basis of optimization of regional educational structures and strengthening of relations between the universities, economy, and social sphere of federal districts. The strategic mission of each federal university is the formation and development of competitive human capital in federal districts by creating and implementing innovative education services and scientific researches. Federal universities implement this mission by organizing and supplying work for large programs of social and economic development of territories and regions. This work includes preparation of qualified personnel, and also scientific, technical, and technological decisions.

The first federal universities were created in 2007 in Southern and Siberian federal districts within the National Project "Education" on the basis of universities and academic centers in Rostov-on-Don (South) and Krasnoyarsk (Siberian). Each university was provided about RUR 6 billion for implementing development programs in 2007–09. Besides federal financing businesses and the regional authorities have been active participants. On October 21, 2009, work on the creation of five other federal universities began: in Arkhangelsk (Arctic), Kazan (Privolzhsky), Yekaterinburg (Ural), Vladivostok (Far East), and in Yakutsk (Northeast).

The National Research University is an example of the new approach to modernizing the education and science sector and the new institutional forms of the organization of scientific and educational activity. Besides additional financing, research universities receive special status that gives them more autonomy. Research University is equally effective in education and science and works on the basis of science and education integration. The major objectives of the Research University are generating knowledge and providing for the effective transfer of technologies in the economy; conducting fundamental and applied research; preparing MA students, and developing retraining and professional skills improvement programs. Research universities should be integrated scientific and educational centers conducting research and professional training for certain hi-tech sectors of economy.

The main expected outcome of state support is the creation of world-class research universities capable of preserving, developing, and commercializing advanced technologies while improving vocational training potential in Russia. Two universities received this status without competition in 2007. Twelve universities were selected on a competitive basis in 2009 and fifteen universities in 2010.

Support for Innovation Activities

The state support to universities was a part of work within the National Project "Education." Objectives of such support were modernizing higher education, implementing qualitative educational programs, integrating science and education, and forming new financial and administrative mechanisms in Russian universities. Support of higher education institutions was implemented in 2006–08 on a competitive basis. All Russian high schools could participate in open competition, representing the two-year innovative educational programs. Higher education institutions that compete for state support from the federal budget ranging from RUR 200 to RUR 1,000 million. The total amount of financing from the federal budget was RUR 5 billion in 2006, RUR 15 billion in 2007, and RUR 20 billion in 2008. Fifty-seven innovative educational programs of Russian high schools got support from the federal budget in 2006–08.

Innovative educational programs provided:

- implementation of new and qualitative educational programs in education practice
- use of new (including ICT) educational technologies, progressive ways of organizing the educational process, active methods of teaching, and methodical materials corresponding to world level ones
- high-quality education within the modern quality assurance systems
- integration of education, science, and innovative activity
- formation of professional competences for graduates, providing their competitiveness on a labor market.

Key Problems and Challenges

Access

Access to higher education continues to increase. This increase was promoted by the creation of new institutions of higher education and by the creation of new courses in existing institutions. The increase continues to be promoted mainly by private institutions. Furthermore, access is favored by decrease in the corresponding age cohort studying in higher education institutions. In 2009 about half of graduates from upper-secondary schools were provided with budget places in universities and other HEIs. Such a situation could raise the problem of inefficient use of public budget. Applicants with low school performance shouldn't be paid for from state budget, as the educational results of such students are much lower.

Quality

University governance also does not encourage any external influence over curriculum and training matters. Hopefully, the Bologna Process and the transfer to a dual degree system will accelerate changes in course structure and content that will better reflect the needs of the modern economy. However, until now many universities have shown themselves incapable of carrying out internal reforms.

Russia places only 50th in the country rankings compiled by OECD regarding readiness of the country's higher education and training systems for the knowledge economy, lagging behind both developed and developing countries, including Finland (#1), Sweden (#2), Denmark (#3), Singapore (#5), Estonia (#22), the Czech Republic (#24), **Lithuania (#25)**, China (#29), **Latvia (#35), Brazil (#44)**, and Malaysia (#49).[1] (Countries in bold have similar GDP per capita to Russia.) In other words, the Russian higher education system has not been transforming fast enough and cannot be considered as contributing to the country's competitive advantage compared to efficiency-driven economies. There is a need to set up vital linkages between universities and the business sector to help diversify the economy in the face of growing global competition and to increase the export of hi-tech products.

Recent international rankings of higher educational institutions have shown unfavorable performance of Russian HEIs. According to the list of the world's top universities produced by Shanghai Jiao Tong University (SJTU) (which includes 500 universities) only 2 universities in the Russia are included in the international list in 2011 ranking. The English Times Higher Education Supplement (THES) university ranking (includes 200 universities) excluded all Russian universities from the international list (2010–11 ranking). This means that quality of Russian universities fall far behind from other foreign HEIs. For example, 35 Chinese and 7 Brazilian universities were included in SJTU list, while the THES list had 6 universities from China (no universities from Brazil).

The higher education system as a whole does not serve the regional needs that have been shown in recent World Bank studies in Russia. Higher education has found itself in a complex situation. According to a recent survey of 890 employers in Russia, less than 10 percent of the people employed by them fully corresponded to the specialization indicated in their diplomas. Research shows that 75 percent of university graduates in Russia have been taking jobs in areas different from their fields of study and most of them have to receive some on-the-job training prior to actual work (Galkin 2005).

Moreover, universal (easy) access to higher education has a serious impact on educational outcomes as students performing poorly in school graduation tests are at a lower starting point during first year of study in higher education institution and have to fill that knowledge gap in order to succeed.

University governance also does not encourage external influence over curriculum and training matters. Hopefully, the Bologna Process and the transfer to a dual degree system will accelerate changes in course structure and content that will better reflect the needs of a modern economy. However, up until now, many universities have shown themselves *incapable of carrying out internal reforms* and experts point to the slow move to the Bologna aims in Russian universities. Because it is excessively regulated and governed from the federal level, this system cannot conduct *research,* take out patents, or establish startups. It is therefore incapable of serving regional needs.

Financing and Provision of Resources

Private funding of higher education has also been on the rise. Between 2000 and 2010, the number of entrants who pay tuition to study in higher education increased both in public and private institutions by 22 and 34 percent respectively. In addition, private financing is increasing due to education loans and grants from the private sector, even though financial aid mechanism is still undeveloped.

There is very little competition between state research institutions for funding. For those funds that are allocated based on the results of open competitions, the current budget code does not allow institutions to sign contracts that last longer than a fiscal year. As the result, contractors have at best six months to implement a contract as the rest of the time is spent on the bidding process. This delay significantly affects the quality of outputs, especially for products with a long production cycle (like complex e-learning materials).

Policy Options

Flexibility and relevance of higher education is the main objective of modernization processes in Russian universities. These issues should be addressed to new educational standards that set requirements to educational process and educational outputs. But implementation of new educational standards should be supported by a total retraining of the university teaching staff. The demand for quality and accountability from students and employers is not strong yet, but it is increasing.

Today, higher education institutions are stratifying into two groups. The first group has strong research and innovation capabilities (with additional federal financing); the second group includes regional high schools, which cannot compete with first group but are very important, particularly for regional labor markets. This process should not stop. Returning to equal financing for all universities—strong and weak—could destroy the first early gains in innovation in higher education over the past 3–4 years. But federal and regional authorities should also think about new problems. What should be the regional higher education system? Should it be the same in each region? Should it be like a big network within federal districts? Administrations of regional universities need to understand the importance of interaction between regional universities, regional authorities, and regional society.

Notes

1. OECD and World Economic Forum ranked 139 countries according to the readiness of their education systems for new economic reality.

References

Abankina, I. 2009. "Impact of Unified State Examination on Economic Activity of Higher Education Institutions." Presentation handouts. State University, Higher School of Economics.
Galkin, I. 2005. "Diploma as a Burden." Russian business magazine N 18, May, 31.
Organization for Economic Co-operation and Development (OECD). 2010. Education at a Glance 2010: OECD Indicators. http://www.oecd.org/edu/eag2010.
———. 2011. *The Global Competitiveness Report 2010–2011*. Geneva: OECD. http://www3.weforum.org/docs/WEF_GlobalCompetitivenessReport_2010-11.pdf.
RIA Novosti 2008. "Research Universities: Perspectives for Development." http://ria.ru/online/155458915.html

Russian Federation. 2010. *Statistical Yearbook of the Russian Federation—2010.*, Federal Service for State Statistics of the Russian Federation.

Shanghai Ranking Consultancy. 2011. *Academic Ranking of World Universities—2011.* http://www.shanghairanking.com/ARWU2011.html.

TSL Education Ltd. 2011. *Times Higher Education World University Ranking.* http://www.timeshighereducation.co.uk/world-university-rankings/2010-2011/top-200.html.

CHAPTER 6

Lifelong Learning

In 2004, the federal government approved the priorities for developing the educational system of Russia until 2010. One of the main priorities in modernizing the system reads as "Development of a Contemporary System for Lifelong Learning." During the years that passed since the government approved the priorities for developing the educational system, certain progress has been achieved in a number of directions.

Condition and Development Trends

Education of Adults (Formal and Nonformal)

Under the former Soviet Union, supplementary vocational education, the system for the professional upgrading and retraining of specialists operational in certain industries, was financed by the state and rigidly controlled. In the conditions of the market economy, the system of supplementary vocational education became completely self-financing, targeting the training of specialists that are in demand in the labor market. In the course of the administrative reforms, many educational institutions for supplementary vocational education were reorganized and united with universities. Today, Russia is practically missing a comprehensive system to monitor continuous education. Mechanisms for recognition of nonformal and informal education are completely undeveloped.

Figure 6.1 presents the share of adults (aged 25 to 64) in nonformal education. Nonformal education refers to organized forms of education that are not part of formal edu-

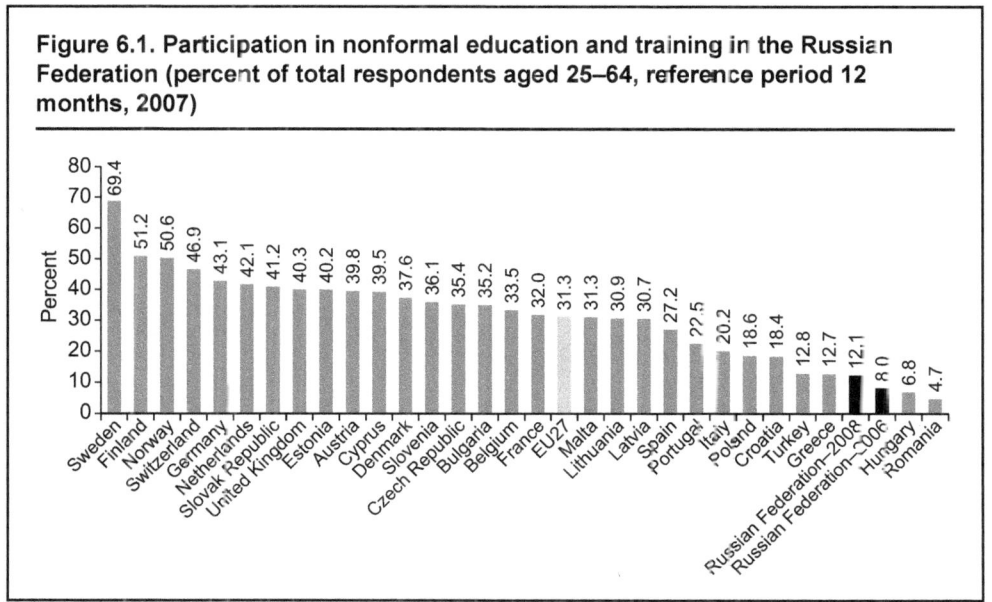

Figure 6.1. Participation in nonformal education and training in the Russian Federation (percent of total respondents aged 25–64, reference period 12 months, 2007)

Sources: Data for Russia: Abdrahmanova et al. 2010. Data for other countries: Authors' calculations based on the Eurostat database, http://epp.eurostat.ec.europa.eu/portal/page/portal/eurostat/home/.

cational programs. There is no data available for the participation of senior individuals (aged 64 or over) in the nonformal education. As seen from the presented data, Russia falls far behind majority of European countries in nonformal education and training.

Figure 6.2 shows the participation of adult population in self-learning. Self-learning in this context means informal individual education that is not supported by a diploma or any other document but contributes to the knowledge and skills. Self-learning may take place through (i) from a family member, friend, or colleague; (ii) using printed materials; (iii) learning using computers; (iv) through television/radio/video; (v) by guided tours of museums, historical/natural/industrial sites; or (vi) by visiting learning centers (including libraries). The data indicates that a very low share of the adult population in Russia participates in self-learning. Only one-fifth of Russian adults participated in self learning in 2008. This contradicts the current situation in the world economy, where technological renovations and demographic trends have accelerated due to the extension of the period of citizens being part of active workforce.

The low share of those participating in the continuous education system can be attributed to:

- lack of intensive technological renovation in many economic segments, which reduces the relevance of training personnel for the employers
- a deficit of educational programs that provide attendees with practical results.

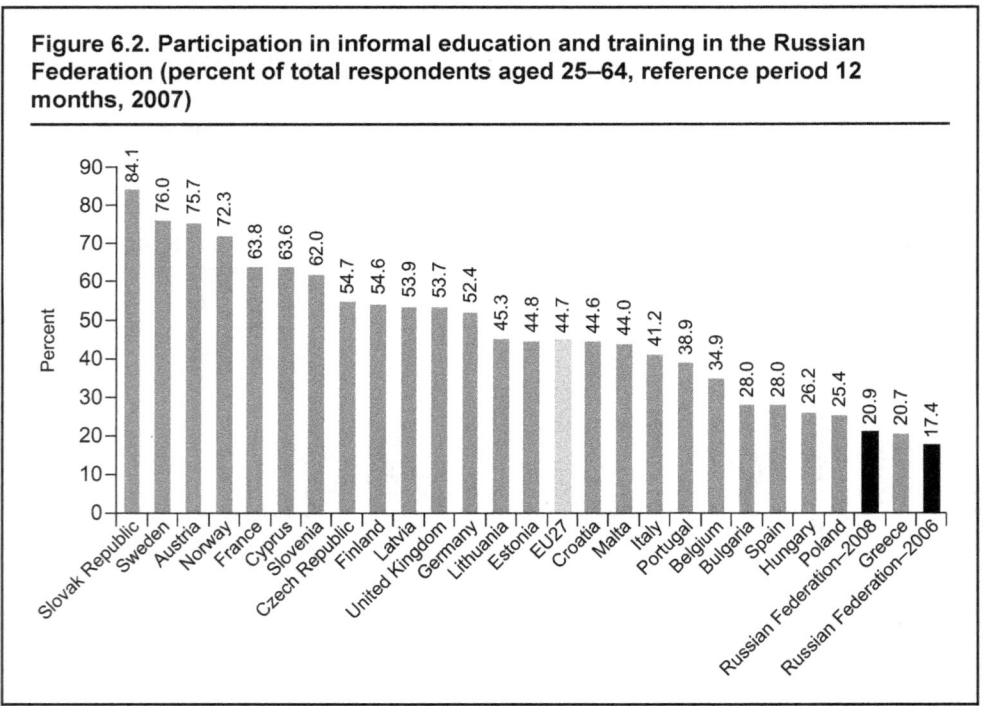

Figure 6.2. Participation in informal education and training in the Russian Federation (percent of total respondents aged 25–64, reference period 12 months, 2007)

Sources: Data for Russia: Abdrahmanova et al.2010. Data for other countries: Authors' calculations based on the Eurostat database, http://epp.eurostat.ec.europa.eu/portal/page/portal/eurostat/home/.

State Policy

Over the recent years, a series of studies in various regions of Russia was held to determine the requirements of employers with respect to qualifications of workforce and graduates of educational institutions. Irkutsk Oblast, Moscow (Shevchenko 2002), Chuvash Republic, Republic of Tatarstan, Saratov Oblast, Perm Region (Kislyakova 2006), Samara Oblast (Shestakova and Konstantinova 2006) and other regions participated. Results of the surveys indicate that the current labor market in Russia, whose main characteristics are flexibility, variability, and highly innovational dynamics, imposes new requirements onto job applicants that were not articulated before. Employers are increasingly showing an interest not only workers' "knowledge" but also in their "skill," "ability," and "readiness" to actually perform the work at hand (Kogan2007). Experts acknowledge that the educational process in institutions at all levels of Russian educational system, on average, insufficiently targets the development of general competencies.

A positive sign in the educational system is the adoption of a regulatory document by the federal government listing mechanisms for the participation of employer associations in the development and implementation of the state policies in professional education.[1] This gives an opportunity to determine requirements for professional education based on the real situation in the labor market and to reduce the costs of intra-corporate training of personnel.

Beginning in 2001, the OECD has been carrying out large-scale activities involving 25 countries to optimize lifelong learning, which, among other things, cover the issue of forming qualifications needed for the rapid response of the working population to the changes in labor market requirements. As a result of these activities, a variety of mechanisms were found to reorganize the qualifications system, which allows improving the coverage, quality, spread, and efficiency of education throughout life. This prompted OECD to begin studying how these mechanisms operate in different countries (Bjornavold and Coles 2010). In Russia, a "recommended" national qualification structure was developed; however no further action was taken for its practical approval or application. Some work has been done to create professional standards and sectoral qualification structures (in nuclear power engineering, aircraft engineering, information technologies, hospitality, and a number of other professions). However, current progress in this area obviously does not meet the requirements for building an efficient adult education system in Russia.

Forming the requirements for adult education within the lifelong learning system implicates that there are active and operational employer and trade associations. The past 10 years have seen a certain progress in this area in Russia. Despite the several positive examples, it must be noted that current social and professional resources are insufficient for a state with significant economic potential and a diversified economy (Pavlova 2011).

OECD countries have a principled stance on the **recognition of nonformal and informal (spontaneous) education** (OECD 2008).[2] Recognition of nonformal and informal education expands the opportunities for adults to receive education in a convenient form, taking into account their interests, their type of work and their schedule. As a rule, actively working people find nonformal and informal education more convenient, or quite frequently, the only possible form of education. Corporate training on the job with consequent recognition allows increasing efficiency of labor, facilitates the introduction of modern technologies, and creates additional capacity in the economy for increasing competitiveness. The opportunity for formal recognition of qualifications obtained as part of the nonformal and informal education stimulates the interest of adults to pursue lifelong learning. Establishing mechanisms for recognizing nonformal and informal education creates an opportunity to discuss potential approaches for their state support.

In present-day Russia, there are practically no resources for independent voluntary certification of personnel. Without such resources, the recognition of nonformal and informal education becomes difficult to implement. Some scattered examples of successful certification centers are available (Yeltsova and Yefimova 2008). Without building up appropriate capacity for official recognition of qualifications, Russia cannot expect the nonformal and informal education sector to have dynamic growth in innovative industries. The experience of OECD countries in lifelong learning clearly indicates that qualification capacity of developed and developing economies will largely depend on the efficiency of procedures to certify professional qualifications (Mashukova et al. 2006).[3]

Staff Training (Financing and Coverage)

A pronounced trend in the development of human resources in organizations and enterprises is establishment of private staff training centers and programs. Research indicates that 66 percent of employers prefer to provide additional training or retraining for their employees on the bases of their own educational departments. Overall, this trend is consistent with the world trend of internal company training of their personnel. However, in Russia this process is of a specific nature: as a rule, the establishment of employers' own educational departments and programs is caused by the fact that organizations (enterprises) cannot find educational programs of required quality in the market (Nesmeeva 2009). An insufficient number of relevant educational programs for adults speeds up the development of inter-corporate training and the creation of corporate universities.

The following approaches to establish corporate universities can be listed:

- Establish corporate universities on the basis of an existing educational center within the company by combining available training programs on common conceptual basis, common physical and informational infrastructure.
- Create a corporate university from scratch by introducing primarily highly technological remote learning programs and by developing new training programs for personnel (for instance, VimpelCom CU).
- Use outsourcing, that is, external providers and the available educational infrastructure of higher educational organizations. For example, the Protek Company uses the regional network of the LINK International Management Institute as the infrastructure for establishing its own corporate university.

Sociological surveys indicate that the share of adults who get trained in recruitment companies is higher than the share trained in the state placement service. This reveals a relatively high activity of private business rendering employment assistance and adult education services. According to the data obtained through sociological surveys by State University, Higher School of Economics, over 95 percent of adult education happens in the workplace (figure 6.3). The presented data demonstrates that the general developmental education of adults is practically nonexistent in Russia. However, by empirical evidence employers often complain that workers lack those (general/basic) skills (Lazareva, Denisova, and Tsuhlo 2006).

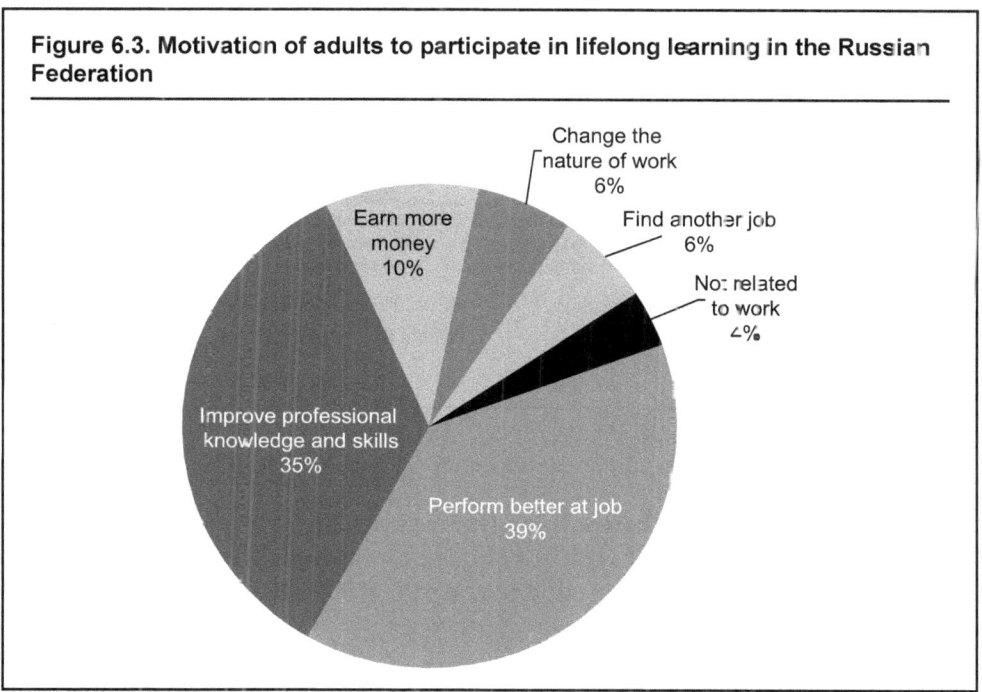

Figure 6.3. Motivation of adults to participate in lifelong learning in the Russian Federation

Source: Abdrahmanova et al. 2007.

As far as a financial model is concerned, standard per capita financing of education is a prevailing concept in the supplementary vocational education programs. This is true for financing professional retraining, improvement of qualifications and training of civil servants, the education of managers and entrepreneurs within the Presidential Program for personnel training, generally accepted approaches to financing target programs training company employees at supplementary professional education programs. The cost of implementation of skill upgrade and professional retraining programs is usually determined by the standard cost of educating one attendee.

Data (figure 6.4) indicates that the improvement of professional qualifications of the personnel is largely financed by their employers, who commit to pay for 40–80 percent of the cost of the education. In Russia, the expenditures of organizations for professional training of their staff, as part of the workforce-related costs, constitute only 0.3 percent according to 2006 data (about US$1.35 per employee per month). Compare this with France, where pursuant to the effective legislation, any enterprise and organization with 10 or more of staff is obliged to allocate at least 1.5 percent of the payroll fund for professional education. The actual average for this number is 3 percent. Expenditure for professional education at small enterprises is seven times less than at large enterprises.

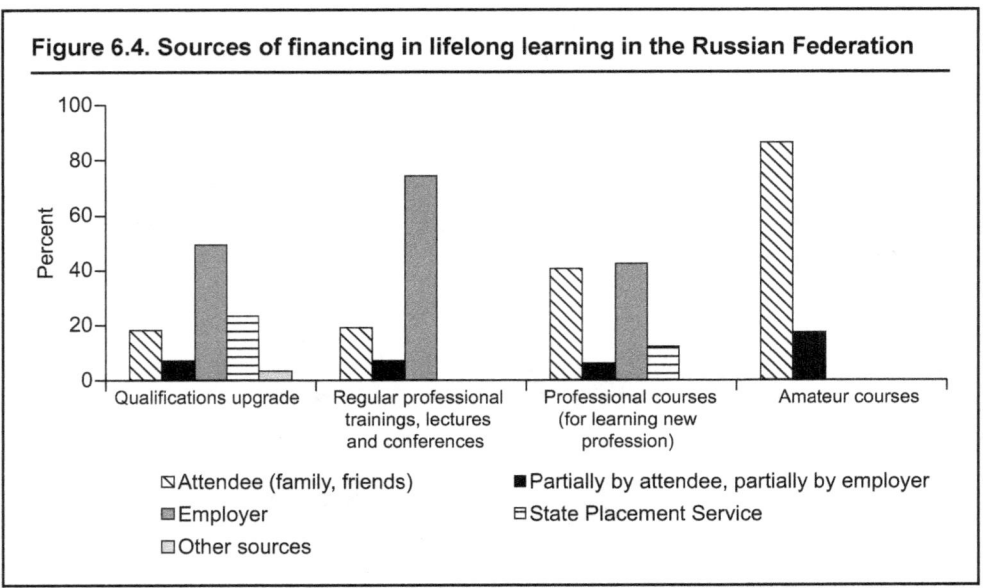

Figure 6.4. Sources of financing in lifelong learning in the Russian Federation

Source: Abdrahmanova et al. 2007.

A probable cause for this situation is the relative instability of personnel at small enterprises, as well as the lack of sufficient funding for the professional education of the employees. Budgetary financing of adult education is at a low level, despite the dynamic growth (figures 6.5 and 6.6).

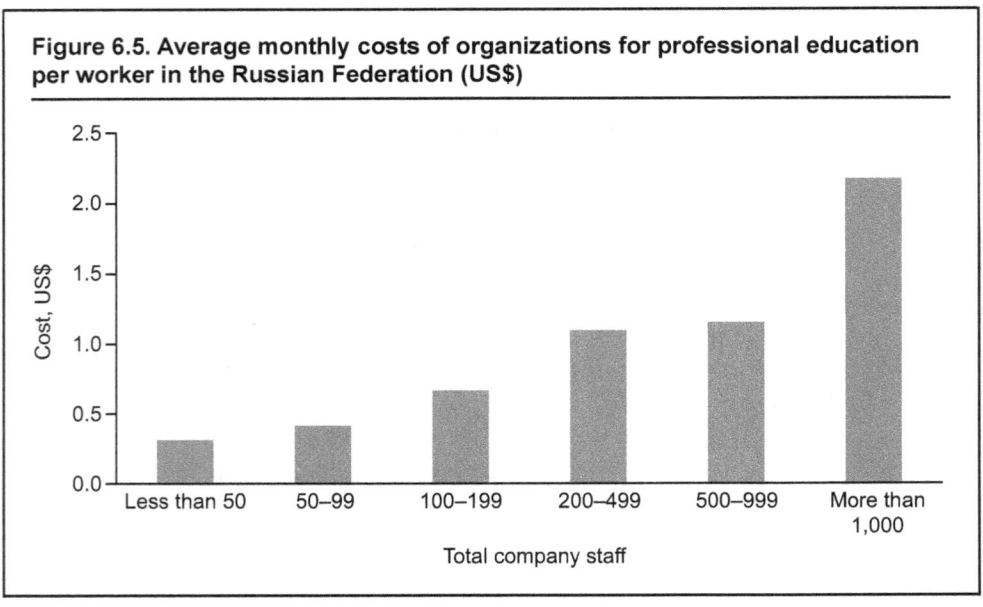

Figure 6.5. Average monthly costs of organizations for professional education per worker in the Russian Federation (US$)

Source: Authors' calculations based on data of the Central Bank of the Russian Federation and Abdrahmanova et al. 2007.

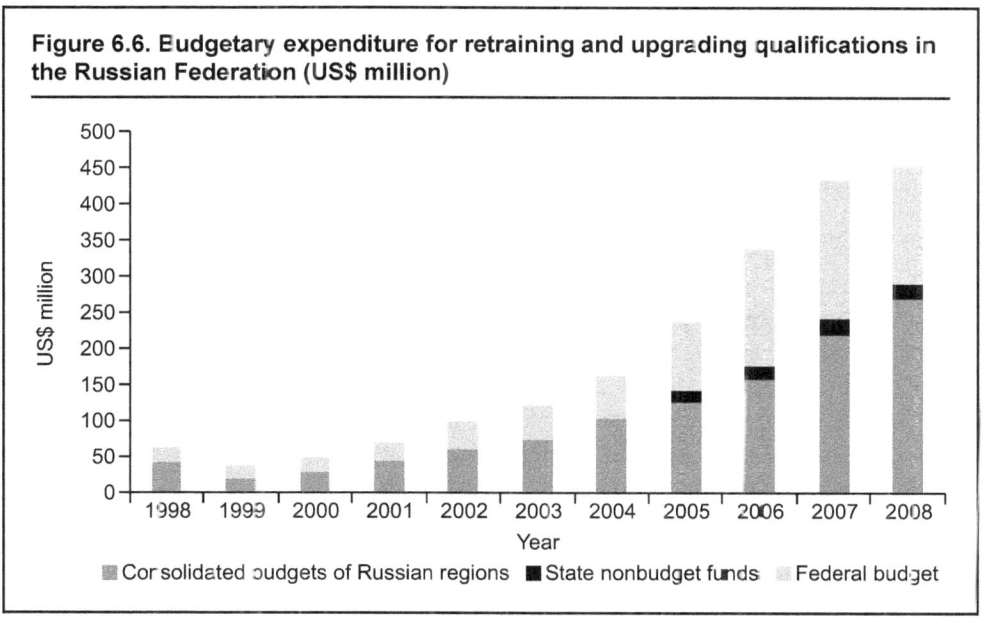

Figure 6.6. Budgetary expenditure for retraining and upgrading qualifications in the Russian Federation (US$ million)

Source: Authors' calculations based on Abdrahmanova et al. 2010 and the Central Bank of the Russian Federation.

In order to incentivize adult education, a new accounting procedure has been adopted in Russia for taxation of employee training related income and expenses. According to new procedures companies' expenses on (re)training of staff are tax-exempt. In the future it is expected that this will have a great positive effect on the intensity of qualification improvement and retraining of employees.

Socially Deprived Groups of People

It is possible to identify segments of the population groups that now have limited access to a system of lifelong learning education:

- **Workers of small enterprises.** Researchers specify that capacity of personnel training is closely connected with enterprise size: the larger the enterprise is, the more potential it has to give training to the staff and the higher its expenses on one-staff-member training.
- **People 55/60–75 years old.** Specialized programs of adults training should include this age cohort in their assessment of economic conditions.
- **The partially employed.** If retraining jobless citizens by the public employment services is a usual practice, then training the partially employed is problematic for the education system of Russia. The partial employment does not give confidence to the enterprises concerning the further prospects of cooperation with the staff. It restricts the specified persons from accessing services of lifelong learning education.
- **Rural.** The educational level of agriculture workers is lower than that of the average participant in the economy. According to researches, there is an abun-

dance of labor in Russia's rural regions. This abundance is not only absolute but also structural. It is obvious that the development of agriculture and a rural social life demands the formation of an effective training system for adults that includes support for finding alternative employment.

- **People of able-bodied age who are not active participants of the labor market.** In any economy there is a gap between number of persons of able-bodied age and number of the persons involved on the labor market. There are persons who would participate in the labor market if there were correct educational courses for adults.
- **Labor migrants.** Enterprises do not have reasons to train migrants if they are not sure that the costs will be compensated. Thus governments of the migration donor countries and the regions-recipients of Russia should be ready to find the solution of this situation. The educational services for professional and social qualifications of workers-migrants should appear on both sides but their standards should be coordinated.
- **Relatives of migrants who did not come to the labor market.** Family members can be motivated, trained, and oriented to successfully enter the Russian labor market if there is a special lifelong learning program geared towards them.
- **Foreign students.** Research shows that students require additional income, which can be organized by partial employment. Such lifelong learning programs should be developed on the basis of educational institutions in which foreign citizens are trained.

Policy Options

Considering the available international practices and the current situation, we have formulated the following policy options for Russia's educational system development strategy:

Establish Infrastructure for Lifelong Learning

- Introduce normative provisions fully regulating the adult education system into the new, integrated legislative document of the education system in Russia (currently under development).
- Develop a national qualification structure based on descriptions reflecting the competencies required for the inclusion of an individual into the practical activities of various complexity, expected increase of the professional and territorial mobility, rapid change of the economic development priorities, need in the regular and rather frequent update of the requirements to the current personnel and results of adult vocational training.
- Create a regional network of certification centers independent from the educational system and specific employers, by which Russian citizens would be able to get formal training recognized all over Russia, as a confirmation of their professional skills. Skill certification should be done regardless of the education type: formal, nonformal or informal. Not only should nationals of Russia have access to qualification certification but the labor migrants should as well.
- Develop and introduce a single scoring (credit) system for primary and continuous professional adult education systems that would allow for a reduction of

time spent by citizens acquiring the required qualifications and would expand their possibilities for structuring their individual educational programs.
- Create conditions for the development of the adult education system integrators (that provide comprehensive services to legal entities), personal tutors and education consultants, mass media specializing in the issues of continuous education development, public institutions on professional assessment and establishment of the adult education program ratings, and the self-regulating institutions in the field of adult education.
- Create a network of methodological support aimed at the development of adult education on the basis of existing intellectual and know-how resources.
- Restructure existing educational institutions of initial vocational and professional education, optimize their network, reject any social or general education functions, reconfigure training programs, transition to the modular principle, introduce a single credit system acknowledged within the system of primary professional education of all levels, and form a network of modern qualification centers providing training for all age groups.

Universities play large role in establishing infrastructure for lifelong learning as they have fewer regular students and excessive capacity.

Develop the Lifelong Learning Services Market, and Saturate It with Quality High-Tech Educational Products

- Adopt regulatory documents, which would enable commercial entities (given the availability of resources required for the educational process) to implement adult education programs including the issuance of state documents certifying qualifications upgrades and professional retraining, as well as a possibility to get public orders for training along with other educational institutions.
- Develop the corporate sector of continuous adult education, which seems promising. In order to develop the corporate education, it is necessary to include the running cost of training centers belonging to the enterprises into the other costs associated with the production and sales. At present, the cost of training in basic and supplementary educational programs, professional training, and staff retraining is treated as other expenses, and only when the training is provided on the basis of contracts either with Russian educational institutions with appropriate licenses or with foreign educational institutions of the adequate status. In order to foster the development of corporate education, expenses incurred by the enterprises for training and retraining their staff within the framework of their own educational programs, as well as the expenses for arranging on-the-job training for students of educational institutions, should be counted in direct production costs. This would be beneficial in terms of reducing the enterprises' taxable basis.
- Assist educational program development. In priority areas of the innovative economic development of Russia, it would be practical for the state to support competitively chosen, corporate education development programs and regional programs for an overall modernization of vocational education. This modernization would have to comply with the social and economic development policies of Russia and the federal subjects.

- Regulate access of foreign operators to the adult education system in the areas where Russia is evidently lagging behind in know-how. At the same time, priority should be given to educational projects that envisage the implementation of the continuous education programs jointly by Russian and foreign operators.
- Develop long-term programs with major migrant donor states to coordinate requirements for these workers' skills and qualifications being acquired in the course of vocational education in migrant donor states.
- Change the priorities of higher education institutions' activities to reflect the higher rate of adults in the training process caused by financial and regulatory incentives. Higher educational institutions should become the major adult education operators updating human resource capacities for high-tech sectors. Particularly, it should concern the federal and the national research universities.

Improve Mechanisms to Finance Lifelong Learning

- Consider voucher financing. Regarding the educational programs financed out of the state and municipal budgets, it would be practical to consider a possibility of transition to the voucher concept of financing. That would allow launching pseudo-competition mechanisms among the providers of educational services for the state budget money. Perhaps choose a supplier of educational services will in the long-run improve the quality of educational services.
- Develop the educational crediting mechanisms in the system of adult education with active support from the state.

Notes

1. Decree of the Government of the RF dated December 24, 2008 No.1015 "On Approving Rules for Participation of Employer Associations in the Development and Implementation of the State Policy in the Professional Education."
2. OECD activity "Recognition of Nonformal and Informal Learning."
3. For instance in Germany a German Accreditation Council (DAR) was established, which is a coordination body aiming to create a common internationally recognized system of accrediting personnel certification bodies both in regulated areas, and as voluntary certification. As part of the Council, personnel certification bodies certify personnel, for instance, in nondestructive materials, welding, plastic process, real estate evaluations.

References

Abdrahmanova, G., Gohberg, L., Zabaturina, I., Kovaleva, G., Kovaleva, N., Kuznetsova, V., Ozerova, O., Shuvalova, O. 2007. *Education in the Russian Federation: 2007*. Annual Statistical Publication. Moscow: State University, Higher School of Economics.

Abdrahmanova, G., Gohberg, L., Zabaturina, I., Kovaleva, G., Kovaleva, N., Kuznetsova, V., Ozerova, O., Shuvalova, O. 2010. *Education in the Russian Federation: 2010*. Annual Statistical Publication. Moscow: State University, Higher School of Economics.

Bjornavold, J., Coles, M. 2010. "Added Value of National Qualifications Frameworks in Implementing the EQF." European Centre for the Development of Vocational Training (CEDEFOP). http://www.cedefop.europa.eu/EN/.

Kislyakova, S. 2006. "Demand by Requirements". *Federal Newsletter of the Kama Region* No. 2 (26): 22–25.

Kogan, Postalyuk. 2007. "Core Competencies in the Structure of Professional Qualifications." In *Qualification Requirements and Qualification Structures: A Collection of Articles*, edited by Volkova, Klimova. M., ANE under the Government of the Russian Federation.

Lazareva, Denisova, Tsuhlo. 2006 "Hiring or Retraining: Experience of Russian Enterprises." Moscow: State University, Higher School of Economics.

Mashukova, N., Postalyuk, N., Nikolaeva, G., Asheulov, Y. 2006. *Voluntary Personnel Certification System in the Russian Federation: Models and Mechanisms*. Moscow: National Training Foundation.

Nesmeeva. 2009. "What Training We Don't Need". JobCenter. http //dps.smrtlc.ru/Disc/training.htm.

OECD (Organization for Economic Cooperation and Development). 2008. "Status of Recognition of Nonformal and Informal Learning in Germany." Bonn, Berlin: OECD.

Pavlova, O. 2011. "Social and Didactic Aspects of Adult Education." *Research and Pedagogical Psychology and Education Journal*. http://obrazovanie21.narod.ru/Files/2011-2_p013-017.pdf.

Russian Union of Entrepreneurs. 2011. "Viewpoint." http://www.rspp.ru/Default.aspx?CatalogId=234&d_no=1843.

Shestakova, Y., Konstantinova, N. 2006. "Green Shot." *Samara Business Magazine for Small and Medium Business* No. 9(25): 2–4.

Shevchenko, D. 2002. "Marketing Analysis of Youth Labor and Education Markets." Journal *Practical Marketing* No. 2 (60).

Yeltsova L.N., Yefimova S.A. 2008. "Certification of Professional Qualifications of Graduates from Pre-university Professional Education Institutions of the Samara Oblast." Moscow: DELO. http://www.interface.ru/fset.asp?Url=/training/borland/sertif.htm, http://www.a-sys.ru/default.aspx?t13=14&t1=2.

———. 2005. "Actual Demand for Skills and Knowledge at Work". Analytical Report, Business Technologies School, Russia.

———. 2005. "International Consortium of Module and Competency-Based Education." Materials of the British Council Project.

———. 2011. "Petrodollar Doping Does Not Help the Russian Economy Anymore." http://www.km.ru/v-rossii/2011/08/29/gosudarstvennyi-sektor-ekonomiki-rossii/neftedollarovyi-doping-ekonomike-rossii.

Appendixes

Appendix A. Reference Statistics—Nonfinance

Table A1. Number of students in educational institutions in the Russian Federation

	1992	1993	1994	1995	1996	1997	1998	1999	2000	2001	2002	2003	2004	2005	2006	2007	2008	2009	2010
Preschool	7236	6763	6118	5584	5101	4706	4380	4225	4263	4246	4267	4321	4423	4530	4713	4906	5105	5228	5388
including																			
urban	5569	5190	4723	4352	4003	3721	3493	3378	3408	3384	3398	3444	3528	3611	3753	3906	4068	4158	4281
rural	1667	1573	1395	1232	1098	985	886	847	855	862	869	877	895	919	960	1001	1038	1070	1107
School	20503	20598	21144	21567	21729	21733	21479	20879	20074	19429	18439	17323	16167	15185	14374	13766	13436	13330	13318
including																			
public	20503	20565	21104	21521	21682	21683	21429	20826	20013	19363	18371	17254	16097	15113	14302	13695	13363	13258	13244
including																			
urban	14444	14501	14873	15146	15259	15238	15049	14581	13998	13471	12783	12017	11232	10497	9940	9557	9396	9405	9502
including																			
primary	180	190	224	250	200	253	244	220	211	210	205	200	192	177	162	148	137	79	74
primary and lower secondary	557	521	513	497	472	448	411	368	338	279	246	217	191	170	158	149	146	177	191
primary and secondary	13397	13456	13782	14029	14136	14134	13962	13607	13025	12572	11939	11224	10400	9811	9301	8960	8826	6267	6303
rural	6059	6064	6231	6375	6423	6445	6380	6245	6015	5892	5588	5237	4865	4616	4362	4138	3968	3854	3742

(Table continues on next page)

Table A1 (continued)

	1992	1993	1994	1995	1996	1997	1998	1999	2000	2001	2002	2003	2004	2005	2006	2007	2008	2009	2010
including																			
primary	269	278	285	291	281	266	250	229	205	190	171	157	135	122	104	113	105	79	71
primary and lower secondary	890	876	877	881	869	850	828	786	740	691	633	578	517	475	449	428	425	434	431
primary and secondary	4830	4841	4997	5187	5191	5245	5215	5141	4977	4916	4692	4411	4123	3928	3721	3516	3361	3140	3049
private	-	33	40	46	47	50	50	53	61	66	68	69	70	72	71	71	73	71	74
Initial vocational education and training	1773	1742	1699	1690	1670	1667	1676	1694	1679	1649	1651	1649	1604	1509	1413	1256	1115	1035	983
Secondary vocational education and training	2090	1994	1871	1930	1986	2030	2068	2176	2361	2470	2586	2612	2600	2591	2514	2408	2244	2142	2126
including																			
public	2090	1994	1871	1923	1976	2011	2052	2147	2309	2410	2489	2502	2504	2473	2389	2289	2136	2052	2027
private	-	-	-	7	11	19	17	28	52	60	97	111	96	118	125	120	108	90	99
Higher education	2638	2613	2645	2791	2965	3248	3598	4073	4741	5427	5948	6456	6884	7065	7310	7461	7513	7419	7050
including																			
public	2638	2543	2534	2655	2802	3047	3347	3728	4271	4797	5229	5596	5860	5985	6133	6208	6215	6136	5849
private	-	70	111	136	163	202	251	345	471	630	719	860	1024	1079	1176	1253	1298	1283	1201

Source: Federal Service for State Statistics of the Russian Federation.

Table A2. Number of educational institutions in the Russian Federation

	1992	1993	1994	1995	1996	1997	1998	1999	2000	2001	2002	2003	2004	2005	2006	2007	2008	2009	2010
Preschool	80317	76674	71714	67031	62867	59065	55397	53031	50647	49253	48232	47835	46675	46518	45696	45151	45607	45346	...
including																			
urban	43027	40861	38029	35962	33887	32004	30311	29082	28187	27513	27094	26723	26458	26420	26119	26232	26770	26833	...
rural	37290	35813	33185	31069	28980	27061	25086	23949	22460	21740	21138	20539	20217	20098	19577	18919	18828	18513	...
School	68270	68478	68634	68970	68799	68432	67889	67550	67063	66833	65662	64466	63182	61497	59402	56407	54259	51657	49469
including																			
public	68270	68110	68187	68445	68259	67862	67321	66943	66428	66171	64979	63759	62474	60771	58683	55710	53568	50977	48804
including																			
urban	19871	20063	20430	20876	21071	21132	21233	21235	21271	21335	21178	21040	20901	20404	20055	19690	19259	18799	18478
including																			
primary	15496	15607	15778	15961	16104	16205	16309	16366	16451	16636	16602	16585	16550	16277	16156	16013	15803	11629	11485
primary and lower secondary	1052	1193	1396	1659	1720	1722	1760	1780	1779	1747	1692	1641	1599	1482	1343	1194	1037	379	330
primary and secondary	1957	1888	1870	1837	1809	1749	1678	1598	1511	1417	1324	1253	1184	1107	1048	988	939	913	923
rural	48399	40047	47757	47569	47188	46730	46088	45674	45157	44836	43801	42719	41573	40367	38628	36020	34309	32178	30326
including																			
primary	19154	19252	19444	19697	19870	20011	20072	20200	20338	20694	20719	20689	20654	20748	20582	20282	19549	18304	17626
primary and lower secondary	16163	16038	15746	15465	15049	14610	14021	13647	13137	12555	11689	10090	0080	8967	7671	5854	5230	3481	7774
primary and secondary	12582	12257	12074	11920	11787	11629	11520	11358	11211	11111	10916	10669	10463	10175	9900	9419	9069	8846	8301

(Table continues on next page)

Table A2 (continued)

	1992	1993	1994	1995	1996	1997	1998	1999	2000	2001	2002	2003	2004	2005	2006	2007	2008	2009	2010
private	-	368	447	525	540	570	568	607	635	662	683	707	708	726	719	697	691	680	665
including																			
primary	-	112	124	141	119	108	82	86	78	68	66	71	68	73	65	65	59	64	64
primary and lower secondary	-	36	34	83	107	97	115	103	97	94	82	76	70	75	73	76	67	69	61
primary and secondary	-	220	289	301	314	365	371	418	460	500	535	560	570	578	581	556	565	547	540
Initial vocational education and training	4269	4273	4203	4166	4114	4050	3954	3911	3893	3872	3843	3798	3686	3392	3209	3180	2855	2658	2356
Secondary vocational education and training	2609	2607	2574	2634	2649	2653	2631	2649	2703	2684	2816	2809	2805	2905	2847	2799	2784	2866	2850
including																			
public	2609	2607	2574	2612	2608	2593	2584	2576	2589	2595	2626	2627	2637	2688	2631	2566	2535	2564	2586
private	-	-	-	22	41	60	47	73	114	89	190	182	168	217	216	233	249	302	264
Higher education	535	548	710	762	817	880	914	939	965	1008	1039	1044	1071	1068	1090	1108	1134	1114	1115
including																			
public	535	548	553	569	573	578	580	590	607	621	655	652	662	655	660	658	660	662	653
private	-	-	157	193	244	302	334	349	358	387	384	392	409	413	430	450	474	452	462

Source: Federal Service for State Statistics of the Russian Federation.

Table A3. Gross coverage by education in the Russian Federation, percent (by level of education, calculations based on full-time equivalents)

	1992	1993	1994	1995	1996	1997	1998	1999	2000	2001	2002	2003	2004	2005	2006	2007	2008	2009	2010
Preschool	52.7	51.3	49.6	49.3	48.7	48.4	48.5	49.8	52.4	53.5	54.8	56.2	57.1	57.1	58.1	59.1	60.0	59.2	58.9
including																			
urban	57.5	56.7	55.7	56.2	56.2	56.6	57.3	58.8	61.9	62.9	64.2	65.5	66.2	66.0	66.6	67.1	67.8	68.1	67.5
rural	41.1	39.1	36.3	34.3	32.7	31.4	30.2	30.9	32.5	33.8	35.0	35.9	37.1	37.4	38.8	40.3	41.5	43.1	42.6
School	83.7	82.7	83.3	83.4	82.9	82.7	81.8	80.7	79.3	79.7	79.1	78.0	76.9	77.0	77.0	70.4	82.0	85.4	87.8
including																			
primary	82.5	80.2	79.9	79.7	78.0	75.4	73.7	73.0	73.3	79.1	84.5	89.2	94.2	94.5	94.2	95.9	97.7	99.6	101.9
lower-secondary	95.7	96.0	96.4	95.4	94.6	94.8	92.5	90.0	88.5	86.0	81.1	77.8	75.5	76.8	79.7	83.4	87.4	92.1	91.3
upper-secondary	45.8	44.7	47.0	49.1	51.4	54.4	58.0	58.8	55.3	55.6	57.9	56.3	51.9	49.3	46.9	43.6	42.0	41.2	46.0
including																			
urban	81.5	81.1	81.9	82.0	81.2	80.9	80.0	78.8	77.9	78.2	78.2	78.0	77.8	78.5	79.9	82.1	85.2	89.5	92.8
primary	78.5	76.5	76.2	76.4	74.8	72.5	71.0	70.2	71.0	76.9	83.3	89.3	96.3	97.4	97.5	99.8	102.1	104.3	107.1
lower-secondary	95.4	96.4	96.9	95.5	93.7	93.1	90.6	88.1	87.6	85.7	81.5	78.2	75.7	77.3	80.7	85.2	90.2	96.4	96.1
upper-secondary	42.5	42.5	45.3	47.6	49.9	52.9	56.4	56.9	53.2	52.9	55.1	55.6	53.0	51.0	48.8	45.3	43.6	42.4	48.2
rural	89.8	86.7	86.7	86.6	87.0	87.2	86.4	85.4	82.9	83.3	81.3	78.1	74.7	73.6	73.4	74.0	75.1	76.7	77.3
primary	92.8	89.7	88.8	87.8	85.7	82.1	79.9	79.0	78.3	83.8	80.0	88.9	89.9	88.6	87.2	87.7	88.4	89.6	90.4
lower-secondary	96.6	94.8	95.2	95.1	96.8	99.4	97.7	95.1	90.8	86.9	80.4	76.9	75.0	75.8	77.6	79.6	81.7	83.3	81.4
upper-secondary	55.5	50.7	51.7	53.1	55.5	58.6	62.4	64.2	62.0	64.1	66.8	58.5	49.0	45.3	42.6	40.0	38.6	38.6	41.2
Initial vocational education and training	28.0	27.2	26.2	25.8	25.0	24.7	24.0	23.3	22.3	21.8	21.7	21.6	21.3	21.0	21.1	20.5	20.0	20.9	21.5
Secondary vocational education and training	34.0	32.9	0.0	30.0	30.5	30.9	30.8	31.9	33.5	33.7	34.0	34.1	34.1	34.0	33.4	33.6	33.5	34.9	38.0
Higher education	22.0	21.4	21.3	22.1	23.2	25.0	27.3	30.5	34.8	38.6	41.1	43.7	45.9	46.3	48.2	50.5	52.5	54.3	55.2

Source: Federal Service for State Statistics of the Russian Federation.

Table A4. Ratio of students to teaching staff in the Russian Federation, by type of institution (by level of education, calculations based on full-time equivalents)

	1992	1993	1994	1995	1996	1997	1998	1999	2000	2001	2002	2003	2004	2005	2006	2007	2008	2009	2010
Preschool	8.0	7.8	7.7	7.4	7.2	7.0	6.8	6.8	7.0	7.0	7.0	7.1	7.1	7.2	7.4	8.0	8.7	8.7	8.9
School	13.1	12.6	12.6	12.7	12.3	12.3	12.2	11.9	11.7	11.6	11.1	10.7	10.3	9.9	9.7	9.6	9.8	10.3	12.4
including																			
public	13.1	12.7	12.7	12.7	12.4	12.4	12.3	12.0	11.8	11.7	11.2	10.8	10.4	10.0	9.8	9.7	9.9	10.4	12.6
including																			
urban	15.9	15.2	15.0	15.1	14.6	14.5	14.3	14.0	13.9	13.8	13.4	12.9	12.5	12.3	12.0	11.9	12.2	12.5	15.5
rural	9.3	9.1	9.2	9.3	9.2	9.2	9.2	9.0	8.8	8.6	8.2	7.8	7.4	7.0	6.9	6.8	6.8	7.4	8.5
private	...	3.6	3.4	3.3	3.2	3.2	3.1	3.2	3.3	3.4	3.4	3.3	3.3	3.4	3.4	3.5	3.6	3.5	3.6
Initial vocational education and training	...	...	...	...	...	...	...	...	12.6	12.8	12.5	12.6	12.4	12.6	12.0	11.3	12.7	...	...
Secondary vocational education and training	...	...	...	17.4	17.5	17.5	16.7	16.9	17.8	18.4	18.5	18.4	18.3	17.6	17.5	16.7	15.8	13.7	...
Higher education	7.0	6.8	6.8	6.6	6.7	6.8	7.0	7.2	7.7	8.2	8.5	8.8	9.0	8.9	8.6	8.5	8.8	9.2	9.2
including																			
public	7.0	6.9	7.0	6.8	7.0	7.2	7.6	8.0	8.3	9.0	9.1	9.4	9.6	9.8	9.6	9.6	9.5	9.2	9.3
private	-	7.6	4.1	4.1	4.0	3.4	3.3	3.3	4.3	4.8	5.1	5.3	5.7	4.8	4.4	4.2	4.8	7.5	7.7

Source: Federal Service for State Statistics of the Russian Federation.

Appendix B. Reference Statistics—Finance

Table B1. Basic reference statistics in the Russian Federation

	2003	2004	2005	2006	2007	2008	2009	2010
GDP (thousand RUR, current prices)	13,243,240,000	17,048,122,000	21,625,372,000	26,903,494,000	33,111,382,000	41,668,034,000	39,063,607,900	44,491,434,427
GDP per capita (thousand RUR, current prices)	91.33	118.23	150.70	188.40	232.85	293.44	275.29	313.54
GPD deflator (2002=100 percent)	111.99	111.73	110.92	109	111.87	113.28	108.8	108.8
Annual currency exchange rate (RUR/US$)	30.70	28.81	28.29	26.33	24.55	29.38	30.24	30.48

Source: Federal Service for State Statistics of the Russian Federation.

Table B2. Expenditures from consolidated budget of the Russian Federation (thousand RUR)

	2003	2004	2005	2006	2007	2008	2009	2010
Total government expenditures	3,964,871,972	4,669,654,367	6,820,644,980	8,375,227,658	11,378,578,092	14,157,027,085	15,847,343,187	17,301,003,607
Expenditures on education	475,572,313	593,405,714	801,768,145	1,036,436,147	1,342,976,553	1,664,203,454	1,777,872,062	1,893,881,917
Expenditures on preschool education	72,082,198	91,695,482	112,998,395	145,343,418	189,681,422	254,545,594	287,153,306	321,348,572
Expenditures on primary and secondary education	236,631,626	298,124,443	355,979,727	475,916,919	599,001,275	737,104,446	795,686,679	827,391,577
Expenditures on initial vocational education	30,371,903	35,591,896	39,439,675	47,437,365	57,592,247	65,545,395	66,846,093	61,660,118
Expenditures on secondary vocational education	24,109,931	30,487,217	43,318,599	55,335,261	70,447,207	93,870,388	102,198,267	102,090,848
Expenditures on higher education	61,161,249	76,963,724	125,880,266	169,911,420	240,240,187	294,571,614	347,220,578	377,778,048

Source: Federal Service for State Statistics of the Russian Federation.

Table B3. Annual government expenditure in the Russian Federation by educational institutions relative to total public expenditure on education

	2003	2004	2005	2006	2007	2008	2009	2010
Preschool education	15.2	15.5	14.1	14.0	14.1	15.3	16.2	17.0
Primary and secondary education	49.8	50.2	44.4	45.9	44.6	44.3	44.8	43.7
Vocational education and training	11.5	11.1	10.3	9.9	9.5	9.6	9.5	8.6
Higher education	12.9	13.0	15.7	16.4	17.9	17.7	19.5	19.9

Source: Federal Service for State Statistics of the Russian Federation.

Table B4. Annual government expenditure in the Russian Federation per student by educational institutions relative to GDP per capita

	2003	2004	2005	2006	2007	2008	2009	2010
Preschool education	18.3	17.5	16.6	16.4	16.6	17.0	20.0	19.0
Primary and secondary education	15.0	15.6	15.6	17.6	18.7	18.8	21.8	19.9
Vocational education and training	14.4	13.6	13.8	14.3	15.5	16.7	19.9	17.3
Higher education	12.0	11.1	14.0	14.7	16.6	16.2	20.6	20.6

Source: Federal Service for State Statistics of the Russian Federation.

ECO-AUDIT
Environmental Benefits Statement

The World Bank is committed to preserving endangered forests and natural resources. The Office of the Publisher has chosen to print World Bank Studies and Working Papers on recycled paper with 30 percent postconsumer fiber in accordance with the recommended standards for paper usage set by the Green Press Initiative, a nonprofit program supporting publishers in using fiber that is not sourced from endangered forests. For more information, visit www.greenpressinitiative.org.

In 2010, the printing of this book on recycled paper saved the following:
- 11 trees*
- 3 million Btu of total energy
- 1,045 lb. of net greenhouse gases
- 5,035 gal. of waste water
- 306 lb. of solid waste

* 40 feet in height and 6–8 inches in diameter

www.ingramcontent.com/pod-product-compliance
Lightning Source LLC
Chambersburg PA
CBHW081940170426
43202CB00018B/2961